A PLUME BOOK

WHEN THE ASTORS OWNED NEW YORK

JUSTIN KAPLAN won both the Pulitzer Prize and the National Book Award for his biography *Mr. Clemens and Mark Twain*. His *Walt Whtiman: A Life* also won the National Book Award. He lives in Cambridge, Massachusetts.

"Mr. Kaplan, a dazzling stylist, is perfectly suited to his subject: what Henry James lovingly called 'hotel civilization' . . . [A] splendid book about a bygone age that has not quite gone away."

—*The New York Sun*

"A subject that proves more revealing of the nature of American democracy than many hefty social and political histories."

—*The Philadelphia Inquirer*

"Justin Kaplan's short but diverting tale of the career of the Astor family is told with gleeful humor and frequent sarcasm. He defines his subject as a commentary on the progression of taste and social attitude—and does it very well."

—*St. Louis Post-Dispatch*

"A fascinating social history as well as a fun gossipy read. Kaplan has an eye for both the dishy details and the deeper meaning beneath them. This vision makes *When the Astors Owned New York* the best kind of history: entertaining."

—*BookPage*

JUSTIN KAPLAN

When the Astors Owned New York

BLUE BLOODS

AND GRAND HOTELS

IN A GILDED AGE

A PLUME BOOK

PLUME
Published by Penguin Group
Penguin Group (USA) Inc., 375 Hudson Street, New York, New York 10014, U.S.A.
Penguin Group (Canada), 90 Eglinton Avenue East, Suite 700, Toronto, Ontario, Canada M4P 2Y3
(a division of Pearson Penguin Canada Inc.)
Penguin Books Ltd., 80 Strand, London WC2R 0RL, England
Penguin Ireland, 25 St. Stephen's Green, Dublin 2, Ireland (a division of Penguin Books Ltd.)
Penguin Group (Australia), 250 Camberwell Road, Camberwell, Victoria 3124,
Australia (a division of Pearson Australia Group Pty. Ltd.)
Penguin Books India Pvt. Ltd., 11 Community Centre,
Panchsheel Park, New Delhi – 110 017, India
Penguin Group (NZ), 67 Apollo Drive, Rosedale, North Shore 0745, Auckland,
New Zealand (a division of Pearson New Zealand Ltd.)
Penguin Books (South Africa) (Pty.) Ltd., 24 Sturdee Avenue,
Rosebank, Johannesburg 2196, South Africa

Penguin Books Ltd., Registered Offices: 80 Strand, London WC2R 0RL, England

Published by Plume, a member of Penguin Group (USA) Inc.
Previously published in a Viking edition.

First Plume Printing, July 2007
13 15 17 19 20 18 16 14 12

ILLUSTRATION CREDITS: National Portrait Gallery, Smithsonian Institution/Art Resource, NY: *top* 1;
Brown Brothers: *bottom* 8, *top* 13; Print Collection, Miriam and Ira D. Wallach Division of Art,
Prints and Photographs, The New York Public Library, Astor, Lenox and Tilden Foundations: *bottom*
left 2, *top* 6, *bottom* 13; Music Division, The New York Public Library for the Performing Arts, Astor,
Lenox and Tilden Foundations: *bottom* right 2, *middle* 10; The Metropolitan Museum of Art, Gift of
R. Thornton Wilson and Orme Wilson, 1949, [49-4]: 3; Museum of the City of New York, The
Byron Collection: *top* 4, 7, 11, *top* 12; Library of Congress: *top* 5, *bottom* 14; © Corbis: *middle* 6; Rare
Books Division, The New York Public Library, Astor, Lenox and Tilden Foundations: 9; Museum of
the City of New York, Print Archive: *top* 10; Museum of the City of New York, Gift of Mrs. Theron
R. Strong: *bottom* 10; Harvard College Library: *bottom* 12; Exclusive News Agency, London: *top* 14;
Mary Evans/The Image Works: *top* 15; Justin Kaplan: *bottom* 15, 16.

Ⓟ REGISTERED TRADEMARK—MARCA REGISTRADA

CIP data is available.
ISBN 0-670-03769-9 (hc.)
ISBN 978-0-452-28858-4 (pbk.)

Printed in the United States of America
Original hardcover design by Francesca Belanger

To Annie, as ever

Contents

When
the Astors
Owned
New York

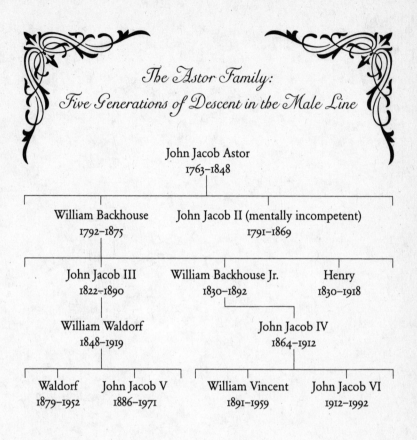

The Astor Family:
Five Generations of Descent in the Male Line

John Jacob Astor
1763–1848

William Backhouse
1792–1875

John Jacob II (mentally incompetent)
1791–1869

John Jacob III
1822–1890

William Backhouse Jr.
1830–1892

Henry
1830–1918

William Waldorf
1848–1919

John Jacob IV
1864–1912

Waldorf
1879–1952

John Jacob V
1886–1971

William Vincent
1891–1959

John Jacob VI
1912–1992

*L*ike English royalty and with comparable pride, the Astors drew on a tiny pool of only a few names to mark and continue their succession. Within the compass of the present narrative, descent in the male line was as follows: John Jacob Astor, the founder, begat William (Backhouse), who begat three sons, John Jacob III, William Jr., and Henry. The eldest of these three sons, John Jacob III, begat another William (Waldorf), who in turn begat John Jacob V. William Jr., meanwhile, begat John Jacob IV, who begat yet another William (Vincent) and John Jacob VI. John Jacob II, the founder's other son, was mentally incompetent and had no part in the succession. Henry Astor, his nephew, was virtually expelled from the family after he married a farmer's daughter.

Prologue

$\mathcal{W}$HEN THE *Titanic* went down in the North Atlantic on the night of April 14–15, 1912, she took with her John Jacob Astor IV. He was forty-seven years old and coheir, with his first cousin, William Waldorf Astor, to a historic American fortune. Colonel Astor, as he preferred to be known, had been traveling with his nineteen-year-old bride, the former Madeleine Talmage Force, who was five months pregnant.

When the ship began her fatal list to port, Astor helped his wife into a cork jacket, led her to a lifeboat, and waved to her from the deck as it was lowered away. "The sea is calm," he assured her. "You'll be all right. You're in good hands. I'll see you in the morning." In obedience to the women-and-children-first law of the sea, he remained on deck and, according to some reports, later repaired to the ship's smoking room for a game of cards. A fellow passenger, J. Bruce Ismay, managing director of the White Star Line, the ship's owner, had jumped without hesitation into the first available lifeboat and rowed away with other survivors.

Astor was probably crushed by debris or a falling smokestack as the *Titanic*, her stern high in the air, sank by the head. A week or so later, a passing steamer, the cable ship *Mackay-Bennett*, picked up Astor's body, floating erect in his life belt, with his gold watch and $2,500 in bills still in the pockets of his blue suit, and delivered it, along with about two hundred other corpses packed in ice in rough coffins, to Halifax. The Prince of Wales sent roses to Astor's funeral at Rhinebeck, New York, in May. The following January a merchantman, traveling along the west coast of Africa, picked up a broken deck chair from the *Titanic* on which one of the victims, whom subsequent myth has held to have been Astor, a devout Episcopalian, had scratched with a penknife the words "We will meet in heaven."

In his earlier years Jack Astor had earned a reputation as a spoiled lordling, deficient in grit and charm; a failed (and abused) husband whose miserable first marriage had ended in a divorce with an admission of adultery on his part. He had also been a public fool on more than one occasion. Although awed by his wealth, reporters who delighted in following his career dubbed him "Jack Ass." His public rehabilitation had begun during America's war with Spain in 1898–1899. He lent his 250-foot steel yacht *Nourmahal* to the navy, donated a battery of howitzers to the army for use in the Philippines, outfitted and drilled his own "Astor" company of artillerymen, and acquired a commission. He saw brief service in the field in Cuba, was invalided out, and returned home hailed as a warrior-patriot. From then on he was Colonel Astor. It was "Colonel Astor," according to a headline, who "Went Down Waving Farewell to His Bride." His death capped his rehabilitation.

Because Astor was the most socially prominent of the *Titanic*'s first-class passengers, his death became a text for an outpouring of editorials, sermons, poems, and songs. Most of them suggested that wealth, whether earned or unearned, was, as always, a sign of grace, nobility of character, and elevated purpose. One song described Astor as "a millionaire, scholarly and profound"; another, as "a handsome prince of wealth . . . noble, generous, and brave." "Now when the name of Astor is mentioned," ran another tribute, "it will be the John Jacob Astor who went down with the *Titanic* that will first come to mind; not the Astor who made the great fortune, not the Astor who added to its greatness, but John Jacob Astor, the hero." "Words unkind, ill-considered, were sometimes flung at you, Colonel Astor," said the publisher and popular sage Elbert Hubbard as he hailed nothing short of an apotheosis of a dead multimillionaire. "We admit your handicap of wealth—pity you for the accident of birth—but we congratulate you that as your mouth was stopped with the brine of the sea, you stopped the mouth of carpers and critics." (Seven years later Hubbard himself was silenced when a German submarine torpedoed the *Lusitania* off the Irish coast.)

Some moralists of the *Titanic* disaster sounded a sour note of social Darwinism. According to them, it had been contrary to the welfare of both the nation and the human race to give over places in the lifeboats to immigrants and other dregs of humanity traveling in steerage. These places rightfully belonged to men of substance in business, culture, public service, and society. In addition to Astor, among such men who stayed behind to die a hero's death were Major Archibald Butt, President Taft's military aide; the eminent English journalist William T. Stead; copper-mining and smelting magnate Benjamin Guggenheim, who reputedly left a fortune estimated at $95 million; Isidor Straus ($50 million), owner of Macy's, the world's largest department store; and rare-book collector and Philadelphia Main Line socialite Harry Elkins Widener

($50 million). Astor's fortune was reported to be about $150 million. (A multiple of sixteen may give a very rough approximation of this amount in present-day dollars: $2.4 billion.)

A few doom-crying clergymen claimed the sinking of the *Titanic* spoke for a judgment of God on a society that had lost its way. They had in mind Astor's divorce, scandalous as well as unholy because it involved an act of adultery; his subsequent marriage, additionally unholy because he was a divorced man and his wife a teenage girl less than half his age; and his earlier years of supposedly unbridled pleasures as playboy, social butterfly, and yachtsman. "Mr. Astor and his crowd of New York and Newport associates," thundered a prominent Episcopalian clergyman, the Reverend George Chalmers Richmond, "have for years paid not the slightest attention to the laws of church and state which have seemed to contravene their personal pleasures or sensual delights. But you can't defy God all the time. The day of reckoning comes and comes not in our own way."

On April 19, just four days after the sinking, the Commerce Committee of the United States Senate opened its hearings on the disaster. The panel met in the ornate East Room of the Waldorf-Astoria Hotel on the west side of Fifth Avenue at Thirty-third and Thirty-fourth streets. (This hotel is not to be confused with its namesake opened in 1931, the Waldorf-Astoria on Park Avenue.) Since the 1890s this monumental building, as glittering an exemplar of the luxury hotel as the *Titanic* of its floating counterpart, had been one of the wonders and obligatory sights of New York City. In the lobbies and corridors of the Waldorf-Astoria the expatriate American novelist Henry James, visiting from England, claimed to have found "something new under the sun," "a realized ideal," "one of my few glimpses of perfect human felicity."

Although temperamentally opposed and otherwise incompatible, it had been two Astor cousins, John Jacob IV and William Waldorf, who together had built the great hotel. For it to come into being they had enlisted a troop of lawyers and negotiators and managed to put aside their lifelong enmity in a single instance of cooperation and suspension of hostilities. As innkeepers (in a loose sense of the word), the Astors had been motivated by considerations of commerce, profit, and personal glory derived from displaying their social eminence and wealth. But they were also jointly motivated by something less measurable: the hotel imagination—a vision of extravagance, grandeur, amplitude, order, and efficiency—that aimed to satisfy virtually all human needs and in doing so create new ones.

Since 1899 a British subject and head of the British branch of the House of Astor, William Waldorf oversaw his vast American real estate interests from a sumptuous London office he had built for himself at 2 Temple Place, on Victoria Embankment. As far as is known, he had no comment for the public, or for anyone else, for that matter, when the London papers carried the news of the *Titanic* sinking and his cousin's presumed death. Their fathers were brothers, and as boys the two cousins had grown up in adjacent brownstone mansions on the same Fifth Avenue block front now occupied by the Waldorf-Astoria, but they were separated by sixteen years in age and had never been friends. William Waldorf— "Willy"—was purposeful and disciplined; John Jacob IV—"Jack"— was pampered and something of a dabbler. Along with blue-blood pride and enormous wealth they inherited a long-standing personal animosity that had divided their fathers from each other and their mothers as well. Willy's mother was devoted to the quiet and upright life, the Episcopal Church, and good works; Jack's had set out to be, and became, the unrivaled party-giver and leader of New York society, possessor, as she insisted, of the exclusive title "Mrs. Astor."

William's silence about his cousin's death was striking nevertheless, since he was the self-appointed historian, genealogist, and spokesman of an Astor dynasty by his time four generations old. Presumably he spent the day of April 15 in his baronial study at Temple Place tending to business and studying his collections of paintings, antiquities, books, and manuscripts.

ONE

The House of Astor

i.

AT SEVENTEEN John Jacob Astor, founder of an American dynasty, left the German village of Waldorf, where he was born in 1763, and came to New York by way of London. Son of a village butcher, he could barely read and write. Toward the end of his life, attended by a butler and household staff who served him on silver dishes, he ate peas with his knife, spoke with a heavy German accent, and was not averse to using a guest's sleeve as his napkin. A visitor from England was appalled to see him remove his chaw of tobacco from his mouth and trace patterns on the window with it. When he first landed in America, for a while young Astor worked for a Quaker named Bowne who bought undressed pelts; scraped, cleaned, and cured them; and then sold them as furs. After two years Astor started his own fur business and traded for furs with the Indians, sometimes paying for their pelts in cut or adulterated rum. He married, and with his wife, Sarah Todd, lived above his shop on Water Street, close by the East River docks. Still a relatively poor man, Astor admired a row of newly erected buildings on Broadway, far to the west of his shabby street. According to Washington Irving, later one of Astor's close friends, these residences were "the talk and boast of the city" because of "the superior style of their architecture." In the time-honored rhetoric of American strive-and-succeed stories, Astor told the author many years later that he had vowed "to build one day or other, a greater house than any of these, and in this very street."

After fifteen years in business for himself Astor was worth about a quarter of a million dollars and moved his family and fur business to a three-story brick building in the row he admired. By then Astor and his network of agents virtually monopolized the trade, but he lived pretty much the way he and Sarah had at Water Street, frugally and without show. He watched every penny, conducted business in a malodorous shop and warehouse on the ground floor, and employed his son William to beat and air the furs to dispel moths. Astor's reach soon became global. He set in motion a trading scheme designed to rack up enormous profits at each junction in its triangular traffic. His fleet of merchantmen were to load their hulls with furs from Astoria, the trading post he established in 1811 at the mouth of the Columbia River; bring them to Shanghai; exchange them there for tea, spices, silks, musical instruments, and fans; transship the goods to Liverpool; trade them there for British manufactures; and sell these in the New York market. Astor believed that his plan to create a commercial empire based in the Pacific Northwest might have made him the richest man that ever lived had it not been frustrated by blundering subordinates, Indian treachery, the War of 1812, bad weather, and just plain bad luck. "Was there ever an undertaking of more merit, of more hazard and more enterprising," he is supposed to have written soon after the collapse of his Pacific Fur Company, "attended with a greater variety of misfortune?" But he accepted defeat with what Washington Irving, who became the appointed historian of the Astoria enterprise, called "his usual serenity of countenance."

"What would you have me do?" Astor asked. "Would you have me stay at home and weep for what I cannot help?"

Astor turned his energies away from the fur trade to acquiring land in Wisconsin, Missouri, and, especially, in Manhattan. He held on with a death grip to what he acquired, eventually about five hundred properties in the city, and watched its value increase at an almost geometric rate. His motto was "Buy and hold." If he had his life to live over again, he often said, and knowing what he now knew, he would have bought up every foot of land on Manhattan Island. The population of Manhattan jumped from about twenty-five thousand in 1780, when Astor arrived there, to about five hundred thousand in 1848, the year he died. Meanwhile and accordingly, the residential and commercial areas of Manhattan had become denser and expanded at a pace that dazzled old settlers. The New York of Astor's youth, Washington Irving wrote in 1847, "was a mere corner of the present huge city." In 1828 Broadway, the city's spinal thoroughfare, ended at Tenth Street, according to the grid plan for the city streets. Forty years later Broadway extended northward to 155th Street and beyond that into the Bronx. Only the three rivers that enclosed Manhattan could limit its horizontal growth. Even though he never did buy up every foot of Manhattan, Astor owned and bequeathed so much property there, prime real estate as well as entire slum districts, that William, his son and heir and a comparably relentless accumulator, came to be known as the landlord of New York. William guarded the family treasure as if he were the red dragon of the Apocalypse.

John Jacob and his son managed their affairs from an office building on Prince Street where each day they supposedly toted up dollars by the tens of thousands. Burglarproof, fireproof, and apparently earthquakeproof as well, the Astor business headquarters had massive masonry walls, an iron roof, doors of iron, iron-grated windows, and heavy iron braces thrown from wall to wall. John Jacob eventually began to live on a scale that more nearly matched his wealth. Standing on the snow-covered Broadway pavement on a January day, the young Walt Whitman watched the great man being readied for an outing. "Swathed in rich furs, with a great ermine cap on his head," Astor was "led and assisted, almost carried, down the steps of his high front stoop . . . and then lifted and tuck'd in a gorgeous sleigh, envelop'd in other furs. . . . The sleigh was drawn by as fine a team of horses as I ever saw."

During the last twelve years of his life Astor enjoyed semiretirement at his country estate at Hellgate, still mainly farmland, on the banks of the East River, near where the mayor's official house, Gracie Mansion, now stands. Looking across the estuary turbulence that gave Hellgate its name, he could see the village of Astoria, named in his honor by the citizens of Queens County in the hope, eventually disappointed, that in return for the compliment he would endow a public building there. When not at his country estate, Astor lived and entertained luxuriantly in his brownstone on Broadway. He filled the house with expensive works of art that the poet Fitz-Greene Halleck, his paid cultural tutor and daily companion, encouraged him to buy. They included a portrait of Astor by Gilbert Stuart, who was then "all the rage," according to a contemporary, and counted George Washington and Thomas Jefferson among his distinguished sitters. A silver plaque mounted on the front door of his Broadway house bore the words MR. ASTOR. Sometimes his servants, black, white, and Chinese, could be seen out on the sidewalk tossing him in a blanket to stimulate his circulation.

The diary of Philip Hone, New York businessman and mayor, gives a memento-mori picture of the eighty-one-year-old Astor at dinner four years before his death, "a painful example of the insufficiency of wealth to prolong the life of man":

> He would pay all my debts if I could ensure him one year of my health and strength, but nothing else could extort so much from him. His life has been spent in amassing money, and he loves it as much as ever. He sat at the dinner table with his head down upon his breast, saying very little, and in a voice almost unintelligible; the saliva dripping from his mouth, and a servant behind him to guide the victuals which he was eating, and to watch him as an infant is watched. His mind is good, his observation acute, and he seems to know everything that is going on. But the machinery is all broken up, and there are some people, no doubt, who think he has lived long enough.

When Astor died in 1848, at the age of eighty-four, he was the richest man in the United States. He may have been the young country's first millionaire, at a time when the word "millionaire" itself was new, before he moved on to far greater wealth. His eventual fortune, an estimated $20 million to $30 million, mainly founded on holdings in Manhattan real estate, was several times greater than that of the nearest contenders in that line, the inventor and industrialist Peter Cooper and shipping magnate Cornelius Vanderbilt. William, the old man's heir, had the body put on display in the parlor of his own house on fashionable Lafayette Place, across the street from his father's. The undertaker installed a glass window in the black silk velvet pall so that citizens who pushed their way in through the crowd of gawkers outside could look upon the face of wealth incarnate.

Six clergymen; Astor's servants, with napkins pinned to their sleeves; and perhaps as many as five hundred mourners, Washington Irving among them, followed the body to St. Thomas's Episcopal Church. Eventually it would be placed in the Astor vault at Trinity Cemetery about seven miles uptown on 155th Street and Broadway. Although entombed like an Egyptian deity, in life the dead man had been nothing less than a "self-invented money-making machine," James Gordon Bennett's *New York Herald* said in its obituary. As portrayed by the press, and as indelibly fixed in the public mind, like the Greek poet's famous hedgehog, John Jacob Astor had known one thing and known it supremely well, and that was "To get all he could, and to keep nearly all he got," as the popular biographer James Parton wrote two decades later. "The roll-book of his possessions was his Bible. He scanned it fondly, and saw with quiet but deep delight the catalogue of his property lengthening from month to month. The love of accumulation grew with his years until it ruled him like a tyrant." This predatory, stony-hearted, parsimonious monster of greed, as he was remembered, allegedly enjoyed nothing better than to count his wealth down to the last penny, drive up tenement rack rents, foreclose mortgages, and put widows and orphans out on the street. For his mentally incompetent son, John Jacob II, he provided a house and garden on West Fourteenth Street and an allowance of $5,000 a year to keep him there. But with the exception of the members of his immediate family, Astor was far from openhanded in the terms of his will. His single large benefaction, $400,000 for an Astor Library on Astor Place, represented less than one-fortieth of his fortune. The *Herald* denounced it as "a poor, mean, and beggarly" figure. Astor left his faithful companion and cultural tutor, Fitz-Greene Halleck, an annuity of $200, so pitiable an amount that

William, although only slightly less tightfisted than his father, increased it, out of his own pocket, to $1,500. William was said to be the author of a widely quoted nugget of wisdom on the subject of wealth: "A man who has a million dollars is as well off as if he were rich."

ii.

IN HIS SEVENTIES, still mourning the death of his wife, Sarah, in 1834, John Jacob Astor had set in motion his last great project. Characteristically bold and ambitious, what he planned was also uncharacteristically self-indulgent and even, surprisingly, a mediocre investment, compared to his other ventures. It was less an act of commerce than one of willful self-commemoration on an impressive scale. Astor determined to put up a hotel without equal anywhere in the world for luxury and architectural grandeur: "A New York *palais royal,*" Philip Hone wrote, "which will cost him five or six hundred thousand dollars . . . and will serve, as it was probably intended to, as a monument to its wealthy proprietor."

To build his hotel, financed from his own coffers on Prince Street, Astor bought up and demolished the entire block of three-story brick houses that had been the seamark of his ambitions as a young man. Although famously close with a dollar, he was even willing to pay an extortionate $60,000, about three times the market value, to get one of the holdout property owners to move. According to a contemporary newspaper account, when Astor learned the owner was still in residence on the transfer date of May 1, 1832, he instructed his foreman, "Well, never mind. Just start by tearing down the house anyhow. You might begin by taking away the steps." Not even number 223 Broadway, the house where he and Sarah lived many of their years together, was spared the wreckers' sledgehammers and pickaxes. For two weeks, as the buildings were pulled down, a stretch of Broadway between City Hall Park and St. Paul's Chapel, the most opulent and fashionable retail street in the country, became a devastation of dust and rubbish, a barrier to the customary tide of foot and wheeled traffic.

Astor's great hotel opened for business on May 31, 1836. After a brief hesitation, during which it was called the Park Hotel, its projector, builder, and owner settled on the majestic and unabashedly declarative name Astor House. Choosing this name gave him an opportunity to offset the failure of Astoria, his fur-trading post on the Pacific coast, as well as the disappearance of "Astor," in Wisconsin, a township tract of land that instead of perpetuating its owner's name was swallowed up by the city of Green Bay.

Two years before he opened his hotel for business, Astor conveyed title to his son William for the token sum of "one Spanish milled dollar." But apart from this transaction, which was intended to avoid death duties, he held on to an extraordinary degree of personal control over the project, from conception and choice of architect to decisions about management, furnishings, and the number of bathrooms. As Hone and other contemporaries recognized, the new building, although only one of hundreds of Astor properties in Manhattan alone, differed from all the others: it was to be the old man's self-willed, imposing monument. Astor House was one of his very few ventures that not only did not make him a great deal of money but could even be called, by his exacting standards, a poor investment: carried on his books at $750,000, Astor House paid out only an annual 3 percent or so.

As model for his venture, Astor had cast a covetous and admiring eye on the Tremont House in Boston, the nation's first hotel built on grandiose lines for the specific purpose of being a hotel, in every modern sense of the word. For the most part, American hotels of the time had barely evolved from roadside inns and taverns in nondescript houses. Their patrons, mainly commercial travelers, had few expectations beyond basic food, drink, and shelter and a bed for the night, preferably one not shared with strangers.

Opened in 1829, Tremont House was a white granite showpiece that gave material expression to Boston's notion of itself as the Athens of America and its marketplace as well. A child of the new age of iron, steam, and mechanical wonders, the architect, Isaiah Rogers, virtually invented the modern hotel: a functionally complex and self-contained structure (and social organization) that was a sort of human terrarium. A closed world designed from the ground up for the specific purpose of welcoming, housing, maintaining, and feeding guests in advanced comfort, the hotel was no longer just a stop along the way: it was a destination in itself, and for some families a relatively long-term residence that anticipated the later "apartment hotel." Tremont House was so innovative that for the next fifty years Rogers's designs, lavishly published in book form in 1830, were the bible of hotel architecture in the United States.

A massive, classically correct building, the four-story, 170-room Tremont House, the largest and costliest hotel of its time, presented to its guests on their arrival a majestic Doric portico, a rotunda with a stained-glass dome ceiling adapted from frescoes in the Baths of Titus, and reception halls floored with marble mosaic. Also on the ground floor were a pillared dining room seventy-three feet long with space for two hundred diners at a sitting, an open piazza, a reading room stocked with newspapers and magazines, separate drawing rooms for gentlemen and ladies, private parlors, several apartments with their own street entrances, and, Charles Dickens noted, "more galleries, colonnades, piazzas and passages than I can remember, or a reader would believe."

Single and double guest rooms upstairs—the $2 daily rate, exorbitant for its time, kept out all but well-to-do private citizens—offered not only comfort, security, and prestige but novel features such as a unique lock and key for each door, an annunciator system connected to the front desk, a bowl, a water pitcher, and free soap. Rogers equipped the Tremont House with indoor plumbing—eight water closets on the ground floor as well as bathrooms with running water—at a time when even the grandest Bulfinch residences on Beacon, Chestnut, and Mount Vernon streets had no indoor plumbing of any sort, relied for their needs on outhouses and chamber pots, and drew their water from sometimes polluted wells in the yard. Some Brahmin neighbors, like the grandparents of historian Samuel Eliot Morison, were grateful to be able to come to Tremont House for a weekly tub bath. By introducing and popularizing convenient bathtubs and indoor toilets, Rogers's Boston hotel, and the public and private buildings all over the country that followed its example, had a dramatically improving effect on personal hygiene. It was also the American hotel, as time went on, that introduced still other mechanical innovations—central heating, gas lighting, incandescent lighting, telephones, elevators, air-conditioning—that became essential features of domestic life in private houses and apartments.

Astor had an infallible sense that his city, not Boston, was to be the nation's social and financial capital, its most cosmopolitan city. New York's rapidly growing transient population, arriving by stage, rail, and steamer, already supported more than twenty hotels. Until businesses and residences moved uptown, Astor's Broadway block south of City Hall Park was Manhattan's prime location, its focus of fashion and publicity, even though, to the dismay of pedestrians and visitors, nomadic pigs rooted for garbage in the gutters while prostitutes, con men, and pickpockets worked the pavements. A few blocks to the east was the Five Points section of the Lower East Side, so desperate and dangerous a slum that Charles Dickens hired two policemen to escort him when he came visiting. During the decade of the 1840s Astor's stretch of Broadway, a promenade and thoroughfare already crammed with shops, barrooms, galleries, oyster cellars, and ice-cream palaces, added two popular attractions: photographer Mathew B. Brady's Daguerrian Miniature Gallery and Phineas T. Barnum's American Museum. In what Henry James recalled as "dusty halls of humbug," the master showman displayed his collection of freaks, monsters, relics, and curiosities, including a "Feejee Mermaid" and an aged black woman said to have been George Washington's nurse.

In the spring of 1832 Astor, nearing seventy, commissioned Rogers to design and build for him a hotel that would overshadow the Tremont House in size, splendor, and mechanical conveniences. He laid the cornerstone on July 4, 1834. Two years and about $400,000 later the noble building he had envisioned as a young man newly arrived in the city opened its doors to an astonished public, which hailed it as a "marvel of the age." Visitors entered a self-contained, virtually perfected world of luxury and dream fulfillment, evidence of what money could accomplish when joined with vision, energy, mechanical ingenuity, running water, indoor plumbing, and Medician magnificence. "Lord help the poor bears and beavers," said Colonel Davy Crockett, amazed at the amount of money Astor must have taken out of the fur trade to build such a palace.

Six stories high, with a Greek Revival granite portico opening onto Broadway, Astor's hotel employed a staff of over a hundred and contained three hundred guest rooms richly furnished with custom-made sofas, bureaus, tables, and chairs of expensive black walnut. A steam engine in the basement pumped water to the upper floors from artesian wells and from two forty-thousand-gallon rainwater cisterns. Anticipating the boutique-ing and malling of the modern big-city hotel, the ground floor housed eighteen shops and served as a marketplace for clothing, wigs, clocks, hats, jewelry, dry goods, soda water, medicines, books, cutlery, trusses, pianos, and the services of barbers, tailors, dressmakers, and wig makers. Lighted with gas from the hotel's own plant, the lobby, public rooms, and corridors, carpeted and furnished with satin couches, became a social focus, a public stage for the display of celebrity and fashion. An immense dining room, with its silver and china alone costing about $20,000, served meals at any time of day or night, a departure from the standard boardinghouse and hotel practice of fixed sittings.* A French chef presided over the kitchen, twelve cooks, a staff of sixty waiters precision-drilled like an honor guard, and a wine cellar that stocked sixteen sherries and twenty

---

*In addition to lodging, the so-called "American Plan," soon offered by hotels across the country, included breakfast, lunch, early dinner, later dinner, tea, and supper and not only every meal but every dish on the menu. Even a down-market establishment like Thompson's Two-Bit House in Portland, Oregon, offered three kinds of meat at breakfast, dinner, and supper. The owners instructed guests to eat up and "get the wrinkles out of your bellies." In a century of gluttony and food bolting, dyspepsia preceded obesity as the national affliction.

Madeiras. The hotel's printing plant, another novel feature, turned out the daily bill of fare. During the 1840s Astor allowed the managers to roof over the open courtyard and convert it into a vast barroom and lunch-counter veranda.

Having planned this hotel to surpass all others in America and Europe, Astor kept his hand on its running. He leased the Astor House—at $16,000 for the first year (he had asked for more) rising to $20,500 after the third—to Simeon and Frederick Boyden, members of the same family group that had made a success of running Boston's Tremont House. He allowed the Boydens to talk him into building seventeen bathing rooms instead of the original ten, but he made the Boydens pay for them as well as for any other improvement or deviation from the original plans. Nothing could be added or changed, not a penny spent, without his approval. When the Boydens' management lease expired, Astor replaced them with one of their clerks, Charles A. Stetson, who had passed the test of a decisive personal interview with him. Announcing that he considered himself "a hotel-keeper, not a tavern-keeper," Stetson went on to explain, to Astor's satisfaction, that a "hotel-keeper" was "a gentleman who stands on a level with his guests." Defining his job in this way, Stetson may have inaugurated the tradition of manager and leaseholder ("proprietor") as surrogate seigneur, in-house Cerberus, and first among equals.

By the time Astor died in 1848 his astonishing hotel was securely established as the best of its kind anywhere. The parents of Henry James had taken up residence there the winter following their marriage in 1840, and they often returned. Henry's brother William, the future philosopher and psychologist, was born in the Astor House, and, according to family legend, Ralph Waldo Emerson, a guest under the same roof, came up from the lobby to greet the infant in his cradle. "The great and appointed modern hotel of New York," as Henry recalled the Astor House, "the only one of such pretensions, continued to project its massive image, that of a vast square block of granite, with vast warm interiors, across some of the late and more sensitive stages of my infancy."

During its almost eighty-year career—a long one, given the fevered pace of demolition, change, and "renewal" on Manhattan Island—Astor's palace, its lobby and sidewalk outside habitually crowded with onlookers, housed the great and famous of the day: Andrew Jackson, Sam Houston, Henry Clay, and Stephen Douglas; Charles Dickens and William Makepeace Thackeray; the French tragic actress Rachel; former president of the Confederate States Jefferson Davis, recently released from a federal prison; Louis Kossuth, Hungarian revolutionary hero, and Grand Duke Alexis of Russia; Horace Greeley and Lieutenant General Winfield Scott, onetime Whig candidate for president, his enormous bulk gorgeously uniformed; Jenny Lind, Barnum's "Swedish Nightingale," who sang to a rapt audience at Castle Garden; and the Prince of Wales, the future King Edward VII, the first British royalty to visit New York. These and others of their kind arrived at Astor House and were welcomed like deities descending to earth. Dozens of papers published on nearby Newspaper Row regularly reported hotel arrivals: James Gordon Bennett told his *New York Herald* staff, "Anyone who can pay two dollars a day for a room must be important." Astor House was to be the mecca and transmission center for a growing cult of celebrity.

Statesman and orator Daniel Webster had been guest of honor at the hotel's opening and always stayed there when he was in town. "If I were shut out of the Astor House," he once said, "I would never again go to New York." He was the towering presence at a marathon Whig Party dinner there in 1837. It began at 7:30 and did not reach its high point until 2 a.m. It was then that Webster rose to his feet and spoke for two hours "in a vein of unwearied and unwearying eloquence," Philip Hone wrote in his diary. No one else on the globe, Hone went on, "could thus have fixed their attention at such an unseasonable hour. . . . I verily believe not a person left the room while he was speaking." Whenever the great man took up residence, and also on his birthday for ten years after his death in 1852, the Astor House flew "the Webster Flag"—a large white banner inscribed with the words "Liberty and Union, now and forever, one and inseparable." Denied his party's presidential nomination in 1852, Webster stood for the last time in the doorway of his suite and announced, his indignation and Ciceronian cadences never failing him although his health had, "My public life is ended. I go to Marshfield to sleep with my fathers, carrying with me the consciousness of duty done. When perilous times come to you, as come they will, you will mourn in bitterness of spirit your craven conduct and your base ingratitude. Gentlemen, I bid you a good-night."

During the 1850s and 1860s, in his parlor suite, "No. 11," on the Vesey Street side, Republican Party kingmaker Thurlow Weed held court. There, his grandson recalled, "caucuses were held, campaigns arranged, senators, members of the cabinet, governors, ministers, and even presidents were made and unmade. For nearly a quarter of a century more political power and influence probably emanated from that little apartment than from any other source in the entire republic."

Walt Whitman was to recall as a moment fixed motionless in

time, the arrival from Albany, in February 1861, two months before
the Civil War, of President-elect Abraham Lincoln. "A sulky, un-
broken, and menacing silence" greeted him (New York City was a
nest of Southern sympathizers). "He looked with curiosity upon
that immense sea of faces, and the sea of faces return'd the look
with similar curiosity. The crowd that hemm'd around consisted I
should think of thirty or forty thousand men, not a single one his
personal friend. . . . The tall figure gave another relieving stretch or
two of arms and legs; then with moderate pace, and accompanied
by a few unknown looking persons, ascended the portico steps
of the Astor House, disappeared through its broad entrance—and
the dumb show ended." From that moment on, Whitman said, he
knew that to paint a true portrait of Lincoln would require the
combined genius of Plutarch, Aeschylus, and Michelangelo. From
the same vantage point on the Broadway pavement near the Astor
House the diarist George Templeton Strong caught a glimpse of
"the great rail-splitter's face . . . a keen, clear, honest face, not so
ugly as his portraits." The thirteen-year-old William Waldorf Astor
also saw the president-elect when he passed through New York in
1861. " 'What a fright,' I heard an old lady exclaim, and certainly
nothing of the heroic revealed itself in that plebeian exterior."

Three years later, during the closing months of the war, eight
Confederate army officers, in civilian clothes and carrying false papers, arrived by train from Toronto. They had equipped themselves with incendiary devices of phosphorus and naphtha. Their
mission was to set fire to the Astor House, about twenty other hotels, and Barnum's American Museum. In the ensuing panic,
Southern sympathizers were to seize control of city hall, police
headquarters, and the military command center and claim New

York for the Confederacy. Along with their firebombs, which simply smoldered instead of breaking into flame, the Confederate plot fizzled, but in theory, at any rate, it made it clear that New York's crowded hotels were essential to its central nervous system and also its richest, most accessible terrorist target.

For all its grandeur and preeminence, by 1875, John Jacob Astor's monument to himself had begun to outlive its time. Compared to the city's bigger, newer, and more fashionable hotels, many of them modeled on it, even the Astor House's famously innovative mechanical arrangements seemed old-fashioned. At first thought by some of the builder's skeptical contemporaries to be too far "uptown" of the city's business district to succeed, it was now too far "downtown" to continue occupying a dominant place in the city's social life. Mansions of the Robber Barons, and the retail establishments catering to them, were sprouting like dragons' teeth along Fifth Avenue north of Forty-second Street. Astor's "palace" had yielded precedence to a newer one at Madison Square, a mile and more north of the Astor House: the white marble Fifth Avenue Hotel, opened in the late 1850s. It offered its eight hundred guests private baths, a fireplace in every bedroom, and the services of a staff of four hundred. The hotel's steam-powered elevator—called "the vertical railroad"—was the first in the city and introduced a radical change in hotel economics and status systems: instead of being less favored because of the stairs involved, upper-story rooms and suites, distant from street noises and street smells and now conveniently reached by elevator, offered comfort and prestige at premium rates.

The Astor House closed in 1875 for the long-overdue installation of elevators, running hot water, gas lighting on the upper floors, and a general refurbishing. According to an 1899 guidebook, the lunch and dining rooms in the Astor House's famous rotunda had continued to attract "on any week day, more representative business and professional men than can be seen elsewhere under any one roof in Manhattan." Even so, the Astor House, once regarded as "a marvel of the age," was a dying venture, victim of what Walt Whitman, poet of million-footed Manhattan, nonetheless deplored as the city's irrepressible "pull-down-and-build-all-over-again spirit." The Astor House closed for good in 1913 despite an eleventh-hour petition signed by five thousand loyalists. The event also inspired many column inches of editorial nostalgia that claimed for New York's Astor House a place in the nation's history along with Philadelphia's Independence Hall and Boston's Faneuil Hall. The last guests moved out, the rotunda barroom served its last drinks and sandwiches, the furniture was knocked down for as little as $20 a room, and work crews began to dig a subway tunnel under the building. It had been old John Jacob Astor's "palais royal," now being reduced to rubble, that spawned what Henry James, early in the next century, was to call "a new thing under the sun," a visible, tangible, and accessible "hotel civilization."

TWO

Town Topics

i.

*P*HLEGMATIC AND CAUTIOUS, the founder's son, William Backhouse Astor (1792–1875), was faithful to two main goals: to protect and increase the Astor fortune and, encouraged by his father, to complete the family's transition in status from immigrant upstarts to native blue bloods. He married conspicuously *up*. His wife, Margaret Rebecca Armstrong, was the daughter of a Revolutionary War general, John Armstrong, later a senator, minister to France, and secretary of war. Armstrong himself had married into the powerful Livingston clan, which, in the seventeenth century, had held the title of Lords of the Manor, major landowners in the Hudson River valley.

William and Margaret had three sons, the youngest of whom, Henry (1830–1918), went his own contrary way and turned his back on his father's social aspirations. After he married a farmer's daughter he was drummed out of the family and effectively forgotten. By virtue of birth and wealth, William and Margaret's two other sons, John Jacob III (1822–1890) and his younger brother, William Backhouse Jr. (1830–1892), assumed a high place in the American aristocracy. In time the two came to occupy adjacent brownstone mansions on Fifth Avenue between Thirty-third and

Thirty-fourth streets, a notably valuable parcel of real estate, farmland not too many years earlier, that their father had acquired at
what proved to be a bargain price. The brothers also shared offices
and, to a varying extent, authority in the family countinghouse on
Prince Street. By right of seniority, John Jacob III was the head of
the House of Astor, his brother what amounted to junior partner,
and this led to jealousy and resentment on William's part. Dis-
agreements over business matters, compounded with fundamental
incompatibility, discordant styles of living, and friction between
their wives, had long since frayed the ties of brotherhood. The enmity between them they were to pass on to their sons.

Imperious and somber, John Jacob III had studied at the University of Gottingen, Columbia College, and Harvard Law School.
Encouraged by his wife, the former Charlotte Augusta Gibbes, he
gradually relaxed from his dedication to thrift, work, piety, and
high morality and learned to enjoy his class's conventional pleasures: vintage claret, fine book bindings, and a villa on Bellevue
Avenue in Newport, where his wife entertained in splendor. A
faithful worshipper at Trinity Episcopal Church, he was also a
force in the Republican Party, despite his aversion to American
politics, which he said did not deserve the attention of a gentleman. Explaining that he had no interest in "public life," in his late
fifties he declined an appointment from President Rutherford B.
Hayes as minister to England, a position that only a man as rich as
John Jacob could have afforded to occupy. His credo, which he
passed on to his only son, William Waldorf, along with scorn for
American life in general, was "Work hard, but never work after
dinner," and the equally joyless "*Always take the trick.* When the
opportunity you seek is before you, seize it. Do not wait until

tomorrow on the supposition that your chance will become better, for you may never see it again."

John Jacob III regarded his brother and next-door neighbor as shiftless, a drifter and wastrel. William had abdicated his duty, intelligence, and education (at Columbia College, where he stood near the head of his class) in favor of yachting, womanizing, low company, Thoroughbred horses and bloodhounds, sullenness, and drink. (He was "a one-man temperance society," said a contemporary, "dedicated to destroying all spirituous liquor even if he had to drink it all himself.") A chronically absent husband, father, and participant in Astor estate matters, he made pleasure his religion.

"Society" was the religion of his wife, the formidable and domineering Caroline Webster Schermerhorn, the city's reigning hostess and clamorously acknowledged queen of New York's "Four Hundred." "There are only about 400 people in fashionable New York," said Ward McAllister, a prominent hanger-on and bon vivant who made the role of arbiter in such matters a virtually full-time job. "If you go outside that number you strike people who are either not at ease in a ballroom or else make other people not at ease." A phrase immediately picked up by the newspapers, "the Four Hundred" passed in to the language as an elastic and convenient label for a small group of New Yorkers held together by a code of manners and a principle of exclusiveness based almost entirely on the possession of preferably "old" money acquired in an earlier generation. Money aged more quickly in America than in Europe, where even the Astors might still be considered at least "nouveau très riche" if not just plain "nouveau riche." The Astors, for their part, looked down on the equally snooty Vanderbilts for being one generation closer than they were to the source of their wealth, the hardfisted railroad and shipping magnate Cornelius Vanderbilt. "Commodore" Vanderbilt had begun his climb up the ladder from a position as deckhand on the Staten Island ferry. "The class which had the money," the historian Gustavus Myers was to write in his classic *History of the Great American Fortunes,* "arrogated to itself all that was superior, and it exacted, and was invested with, a lordly deference. It lived in the finest mansions and laved in luxury. Surrounded with an indescribably pretentious air of importance, it radiated tone, command, and prestige."

The *New York Times* and other papers routinely supplied readers with guest lists, menus, and other details of Mrs. Astor's notoriously long and dull parties. A typical midnight supper menu in her mansion on Fifth Avenue offered, among main courses served on plates of silver and gold, terrapin, fillet of beef, canvasback duck, partridge with truffles, quail, game, and foie gras in aspic. Pyramids of hothouse fruit and banks of orchids, roses, apple blossoms, and azaleas decorated her table and dining room. As many as 125 outside caterers supported a resident staff of eighteen. The Astor servants wore court livery: green plush coats, white knee breeches, black silk stockings, gold buckles, and red whipcord vests with brass buttons stamped with the coat of arms and motto that the William Astors had awarded themselves, *Semper Fidelis.* (In keeping with this heraldic dignity, Caroline prevailed on her husband to drop or at least mute his middle name, Backhouse, because of its demeaning associations with privies.) Wearing a black wig to cover her graying hair, Caroline received her guests standing in front of the full-length portrait (now in the Metropolitan Museum of Art) she had commissioned from the fashionable French academician Emile Carolus-Duran. This was her official portrait, and she discouraged the display of other images of herself. She favored royal purple in her velvets, satins, and silks and was an indispensable source of copy for the daily papers and especially for *Town Topics,* Colonel William A. D'Alton Mann's weekly gossip sheet. His genius for nosing out scandal and skating along the edges of outright extortion earned him a comfortable living and a fearsome eminence. The colonel (he had won his rank in the Civil War) made it his profession either to publish or to withhold on proper payment (for accounting purposes politely carried as a "loan") highly spiced news items of concern to members of society.

At her last formal reception in 1905, *Town Topics* reported, Mrs. Astor "wore a massive tiara that seemed a burden upon her head, and she was further weighed down by an enormous dog collar of pearls with diamond pendant attachments. She also wore a celebrated Marie Antoinette stomacher of diamonds and a large diamond corsage ornament. Diamonds and pearls were pinned here and there about the bodice. She was a dozen Tiffany cases personified." She had a court chamberlain, Harry Lehr, a butterfly who had made his social debut in Baltimore as a female impersonator and was now a commission wine salesman on the side. Lehr said his mistress looked like "a walking chandelier." Toward the end of her life (she died in 1908) Caroline began to bend with the more liberal times and even ventured out of her palace to make a public appearance by dining at Sherry's Restaurant on Fifth Avenue at Thirty-seventh Street. This "event," as the gossip pages recognized it to be, caused almost as much consternation as if she had been seen tucking into the free lunch of pigs' knuckles and hard-boiled eggs at Steve Brodie's Bowery Saloon. She joked that she had begun to spice up her usual dinner guest list, long on bloodlines and bloated bank accounts and notably short on wit and intellect, by inviting a few "bohemians" off the street. She said she had in mind J. P. Morgan and Edith Wharton.

Caroline was determined to be known to society, the United States postal system, and the world at large simply as "Mrs. Astor," sole, generic, needing no forename, and tolerating no competition for that title from her nephew's wife, who of course was also a "Mrs. Astor." Caroline's husband seemed uninterested in his wife's guests and preferred to live far away from the stupefying and gluttonous tumult of her balls and dinner parties. He was generally to be found in Europe and Florida; at Ferncliff, his country estate at Rhinebeck on the Hudson; or, with female guests, both social and professional, aboard *Ambassadress,* the biggest yacht afloat. He eventually replaced it with the more sumptuous 250-foot all-steel *Nourmahal,* meaning "Light of the Harem." When asked about her husband's absences, Caroline would reply placidly, as Elizabeth Lehr, Harry's wife, reported, "Oh, he is having a delightful cruise. The sea air is so good for him. It is a great pity I am such a bad sailor, for I should so much enjoy accompanying him. As it is, I have never even set foot on the yacht."

In 1890 John Jacob III died of heart disease in his Fifth Avenue mansion, and two years later William Backhouse died of a ruptured aneurysm in a Paris hotel suite. Their sons inherited their differences and genetic incompatibility. William Waldorf Astor and John Jacob Astor IV, sixteen years younger, scarcely knew but disliked and resented each other all the same and rarely met. The immense wealth each of them inherited conferred on them the status of crown princes in a society without a throne: William Waldorf's stake, estimated at his death at $150 million to $300 million, made him (said the *New York Times*) "the wealthiest man in America, if not the world." However much these princes sought privacy, their wealth made them de facto public figures, especially vulnerable to comment because the Astors, along with the trustees of Trinity Church, were the city's major slumlords. They drew rent money from festering tenements that harbored three-quarters of the city's population in conditions that put Calcutta to shame. An unspoken but iron code exposed Astor scions to scrutiny and abuse by the newspapers, as well as envy and suspicion, if not downright hostile regard at every turn. That code held them accountable not only for how they used their wealth and how it had been gotten but also the degree, if at all measurable, to which they had deserved to possess it in the first place. They were in debt to their money, even captives of it, but any complaints from them on that score invited ridicule as "unhappy millionaires."

Relatively few career choices outside of banking and the law were open to most members of New York's moneyed upper class. They practiced these professions in a part-time, gentlemanly way and were mainly occupied with conserving rather than expanding their family interests. "Even the acquiring of wealth," Edith Wharton recalled of New York's "old money" families, "had ceased to interest the little society into which I was born. In the case of some of its members, such as the Astors and Goelets, great fortunes, originating in a fabulous increase of New York real estate values, had been fostered by judicious investments and prudent administration, but of feverish money-making, in Wall Street or in railway, shipping or industrial enterprise, I heard nothing in my youth." If, as rarely happened, a very rich man such as William Waldorf Astor chose to enter politics and public life instead of living a life of leisure, he was likely to find that derision, resentment, and suspicion were the price of entrance. "A wealthy man," Tocqueville had written in the 1830s, "would think himself in bad repute if he employed his life solely in living. It is for the purpose of escaping this obligation to work that so many rich Americans come to Europe, where they find some scattered remains of aristocratic society, among whom idleness is still held in honor." In a society that, unlike Europe, had no tolerance for "idleness" and no commonly accepted concept of leisure ("the nonproductive consumption of time," in Thorstein Veblen's definition), wealth alone could condemn its possessors to dwindle into playboys, "clubmen," sportsmen, alcoholics, expatriates, and eccentrics who pursued amusement and novelty to allay their boredom, lassitude, and inertia.

After his father's death, John Jacob Astor IV, then twenty-eight, kept a close and knowing eye on the management of his share of the Astor estate, but this took up only a tiny portion of his time. He belonged to about two dozen clubs in New York, Tuxedo Park, and Newport and "divided his time" (in the idiom of society news reporting) between his yacht, his Fifth Avenue mansion, his country estate at Rhinebeck, a seasonal "cottage" at Newport, and other residences. "The wilfully idle man, like the wilfully barren woman," Theodore Roosevelt declared, managing somehow to conflate birth control and leisure, "has no place in a sane, healthy, vigorous community." Roosevelt's hyperenergized personality prevailed over the popular prejudice against blue bloods entering the hurly-burly of politics, but in this respect, as well as in so many others, he was an exception. For the two Astor cousins, neither of them outgoing, empathetic, or philanthropic in his makeup, it was nearly impossible to find a comfortable "place" in American life outside the family countinghouse. "We were too prosperous," William recalled toward the end of his life. "We liked the amenities of foreign travel; we had been known to employ alien servants, French chefs and English butlers. We were un-American."

ii.

GEORGE TEMPLETON STRONG, diarist, civic leader, and Trinity Church vestryman, was often a guest at the dinner table of John Jacob Astor III. Over nearly a decade he recorded his impressions of his host's only child, William Waldorf, born in 1848, the year of the founding Astor's death. "Has shot up too fast and looks delicate and fragile. He seems a nice, well mannered boy of eighteen, more or less," Strong wrote. Nearing twenty-one, an accomplished fencer and boxer, Willy was "not handsome," the diarist noted a few years later, "but well-bred, modest, self-possessed, and agreeable. He inherits something of his mamma's refined, courteous manner." Another few years later, after Willy had returned from a stay in Germany and Italy, Strong called him "a nice, refined young fellow" who showed significant artistic talent and initiative—"His statue, 'The Wounded Amazon,' is a creditable work." Willy had made at least, a maquette of this ambitious standing figure while studying under the renowned expatriate sculptor William Wetmore Story. Story's apartment in the Palazzo Barberini in Rome was one of the centers of artistic life for Willy and other Americans.

At the age of twenty-six, when he made his last appearance in Strong's diary, "nice young Willy Astor" was an imposing figure, athletic, over six feet tall, with polished manners, an intense and unflinching gaze, and a worldly assurance that belied his essential shyness and melancholy. Fluent in French, German, and Italian, he had by then graduated from Columbia Law School, been taken into the Astor estate "Counting Room" at 85 Prince Street, passed the bar, clerked in the law office of the attorneys for the estate, and acquired a command of real estate law and business practice, along with a measure of aplomb.

Sent once on a business errand to Boston, he had time for a cultural visit to Cambridge. There William Dean Howells, then an *Atlantic Monthly* editor, took him to meet a famous neighbor, Henry Wadsworth Longfellow, "the most beautiful old man I have ever seen," Astor was to recall. The fame of the family real estate millions, and of how they were acquired, had preceded young Willy Astor to the Longfellow house on Brattle Street, and the poet put to him a question that he said had been "long in my thoughts." "Frankly, when you foreclose a mortgage, do you not feel some compunction for a fellow creature?" Willy had learned his business well at the Counting Room on Prince Street. Compunction? "No," he answered. "We could never feel the emotion you suggest, because we are not taking the Mortgagor's money from him but our own." "The great man listened dubiously," his visitor recalled, "and turned the talk to other things."

"In boyhood," Astor wrote toward the end of his life, "I was taught that I and the Estate would some day be one and that my life would be judged by my success or failure in its control. . . . My business education began on simple lines. I was instructed in double-entry bookkeeping. With a pocket map-book I was taken to inspect our real estate scattered in little patches from the Battery to Harlem. I was taught the art and mystery of coupon-clipping and in my time must have cut a barrelful of coupons. . . . I did the work in turn of every junior member of the office staff." Serious, well trained, and conspicuously intelligent, he had a passion for art and history but appeared to be obediently headed for a life of duty much like his father's and grandfather's, as guardian and multiplier of old John Jacob Astor's high-piled wealth and pillar of the American upper class.

"I was myself brought up severely and kept upon a pitiful allowance," William recalled. "I lived in an atmosphere of sinister religion filled with hobgoblins. . . . I was a mischievous little animal and everybody kept telling me I was so bad. The hellfire sermons of my childhood, the like of which no congregation out of Scotland would listen to today, frightened me silly and I knew those red hot things were being made ready for *me*." Even in his mature years he was sometimes oppressed by the theological gloom of his boyhood in his parents' somber mansion. "Sunday was a day of penance. My Mother fixed the employment of the hours left free between morning and afternoon service. No exercise, nor game, nor merriment. To walk (except to Church) was Sabbath breaking, to whistle a tune, sin. To write a letter, or pay a visit, or read a newspaper or listen to music was desecration. Apart from Church, it must be a day of idle vacuity. 'I see no reason,' she said, 'why a Christian should not be cheerful,' a phrase which now sounds ridiculous. She was proficient in the Christian doctrine of sin." Many years later, leaving church after a Sunday service, he once said to his daughter Pauline (as she recalled), "I can never understand how we can thank God for our creation."

Brought up by governesses in the absence of a more than ceremonial and devotional relationship with his parents, educated at home by private tutors before he was enrolled at Columbia Grammar School, restricted in his reading to history and biography of an improving sort, Willy had grown up companionless. All his life he was to be torn between warring natures: the one romantic, artistic, and solitary; the other obedient to the principle of order, discipline, piety, and control that was part of his heritage. An expert chess player, he trained his memory by playing blindfolded and said the game had taught him "that in all things concentration is the key to success." In later life Willy's shyness and sensitivity often took the protective forms of truculence, impulsiveness, and a thickening crust of self-reserve. His chess-disciplined nature showed itself in obsessive personal habits. He demanded that his desk pencils be arranged with parade-ground precision.

Despite the Calvinist rigors of his upbringing, during the time abroad that his parents allowed him—at the university in Gottingen and then in Italy—the more open side of his nature flourished. Willy developed an educated and acquisitive passion for Renaissance art and classical antiquities. He studied the lives of Napoleon Bonaparte, the Borgias, and the Sforzas and believed he could make a name for himself as an author of historical novels and stories.

In Italy, when he was twenty-one, he had what he called "a love adventure . . . with a young lady of rare charm." "She was a figure of statuesque beauty. It was a strange and delicious emotion, an intense dreaming and anguish," he wrote in a letter in 1904 when he was fifty-six. "I became humanized and lifted out of my youthful savagery. . . . But the fates were unkind and we were not allowed to marry." In all likelihood his parents summoned him home once they learned of the potential misalliance of the Astor millions with an Italian girl who was unknown to them and probably a Roman Catholic as well. But he continued to ask himself, "Had we been allowed to marry, would life have been happiness for us both?" In "A Secret of Olympus," a story he published in his

Pall Mall Magazine in November 1904, Willy wrapped his Italian love in a mantle of operatic prose. "Her dark eyes looked golden in the noonday, like yellow catseyes, and as she smiled her teeth showed white as fresh-cut ivory. Yet across her face floated a swift tinge of tragic passion—as unfathomable as the depth that lurks between the rose leaves. . . . I shall never again behold her; but now Time, with a thrill akin to rich accords of music, weaves for me an exquisite witchery about those happy days." Toward the end of Willy's story, the girl begs him to go away with her, "where none can find us." "Our hands had met; and how often in after years . . . have I asked myself, would it have been well for us if that hand-clasp had been for life."

Who the girl was he never said, but he remained in touch with her—his "princess"—until she died in 1909. "We walked forty years in unaltered friendship, till by a singular coincidence forty years to a day from our first meeting the eyes I had loved closed forever." With a lasting and chastening sense of regret about this road not taken, Willy returned to America, to his prescribed duties in the Astor estate office, and to an existence bounded by the conventions of his social class. In 1878, when he was thirty, he married Mary "Mamie" Dahlgren Paul of Philadelphia, a notable beauty who was endowed with the warmth and spontaneity he had never experienced with his parents. Although it may have lacked the high passion of his Italian affair, it was nevertheless a love marriage, happy and genuinely affectionate as well as socially impeccable. Willy and Mamie were to be the parents of five children (only three of whom—Waldorf, John, and Pauline—lived to adulthood). Meanwhile, they entertained grandly and generously in the house at 4 East Thirty-third Street that had been his father's wedding gift to them, a country house on Long Island, and a rented estate at

Newport. Despite Mamie's ingrained reticence and gentleness, Willy urged her, although without much success, to enter into open competition with his aunt Caroline for New York and Newport social primacy.

Willy's tastes and habits did not run to horses, yachts, cards, and similar pleasures enjoyed by members of his social class. He took a different route altogether. The summer before his marriage, as he recalled, "I startled and amused my relatives by declaring my wish to stand for election to the New York State Legislature, a body endowed with infinite power for mischief." In his letter accepting nomination, he declared his "devotion to the principles of the Republican Party, the maintenance of law and order, equal rights for all, and honest money." His four-year sally into politics, a departure from the customary pursuits of young men of his class, took him from assemblyman to state senator and then to an unsuccessful run for the House of Representatives in the Seventh Congressional District, a Tammany-dominated area that included blocks of Astor tenements. Until then he had been a modest favorite of the *New York Times,* for one, which had praised him in editorials for his diligence, "thorough study of the law," and "fidelity to public interests." After his narrow defeat—by 165 out of over 23,000 votes—the paper turned on him for his "ignoble subservience to [the] machine dictation" of Republican Party boss Roscoe Conkling, dispenser of political spoils and enemy of civil service reform. "The moral is that the possessor of an honored name, of great wealth, of sound ability, and of an unexceptionable private character may throw all these advantages away when at a critical moment in his political career he forgets what is due to his constituents as well as to his own independence and self-respect."

The *New York Sun* wrote him off as "partisan," "narrow-minded," and "selfish," with nothing to recommend him except his money.

Embittered by his defeat and by similar denunciations on other editorial pages, Willy withdrew from politics and to the end of his days fed his rage on hatred of the American press—"tobacco-spitting journalism," an "atrocity" that "trained vulgarians" inevitably visited upon men of wealth, education, breeding, and social standing. He looked back on his political career as "a fine roll in the mire—unfamiliar streets, outlandish slums, villainous drinking saloons, Negroes trying to be white, speeches inane, humorous, half mad." In his rage and disappointment he overlooked something all too obvious to his campaign managers and the electorate. By upbringing and temperament William Waldorf Astor had been unsuited from the start for what he considered the shabby business of canvassing saloons, dance halls, breweries, and tobacco shops. This proud Astor had been compelled to play the part of suppliant, like Shakespeare's Coriolanus, and stand at the city gates, hat in hand, begging citizens for their votes while recoiling from their touch and smell.

On his election-eve swings through the city's saloons he dutifully handed out cigars, put $20 gold pieces on the bar, and ordered whiskey and beer all around. He said a few accommodating words, sometimes in German, about the family roots in Baden, when he toured the beer gardens. Going against the advice of his handlers, he refused to canvass the tenements. Impeccably dressed and hatted, he kept his gloves on when he shook hands and barely sipped his drink before making a quick exit. His closed carriage, drawn by matched bay horses, waited at the door.

. . .

A year before his defeat and exit from politics William began to turn over in his mind what he called his "English Plan." "On the 20th day of September 1880, when I was 32, the thought occurred to me that we should fare better in another land." Soon after, an ideal if only temporary solution to his unhappiness in America presented itself. In August 1882, Republican president Chester A. Arthur appointed him envoy extraordinary and minister plenipotentiary to Italy. "Go and enjoy yourself, my dear boy," the president told him. "Have a good time!" Secretary of State Frederick Frelinghuysen offered a similar instruction. "Young man, don't write me many dispatches."

With only nominal duties connected with the position, Willy was free now to lead the life of cultivated, guiltless, and studious leisure denied him back home. He and Mamie rented and took up residence in the enormous Palazzo Rospigliosi, entered Roman society, gave lavish parties, and quickly became court favorites of King Umberto and Queen Margharita. The queen pronounced Minister Astor's wife "the most beautiful woman in Italy." Willy returned to the passions of his youth, sculpture, drawing, and studies in Italian art and history.

He wrote a novel about Cesare and Lucrezia Borgia, *Valentino: An Historical Romance of the Sixteenth Century in Italy,* published by Scribner's in 1885. "In Rome, on a crisp December morning in the year 1501," it began, "Monsignor Roccamura, Governor-General and Prelate of the Castle of St. Angelo, stood at the rampart of that fortress gazing upon the eddying Tiber at his feet, upon the houses opposite, and upon the Alban hills stretching away southward in varying tints of verdure." Four years later he followed this romantic effusion with a similarly atmospheric costume drama, *Sforza, a Story of Milan,* set in 1499 and also published by Scribner's. "At the half-finished Duomo, the people streamed in and out, pausing in the cool, incensed air of the aisles to touch a finger in holy water." Contrary to his expectations, neither book, for all their fashionable romantic lushness, made him a name as a popular novelist.

In a discriminating, informed, and also wholesale way, using the almost limitless wealth at his disposal, William had begun what was to be a lifelong career as collector on an epic scale. Over the years he amassed books, manuscripts, autographs, Pompeian relics, coins, tapestries, armor, crossbows, halberds, classical and Renaissance statuary and sculpture, ecclesiastical vestments, Shakespeare folios. Instead of the French impressionists American millionaires were beginning to take back home with them, he bought paintings by early masters such as Holbein and Clouet. Among his miscellaneous artifacts were a seventeenth-century New England spinning wheel and a hat once worn by Napoleon, one of his heroes, along with the princes and condottieri of Renaissance Italy. He planned in time to install his collections in palaces of his own: the cream-colored chateau he was soon to put up next door to Collis Huntington's mansion on Fifth Avenue and Fifty-sixth Street, the fortresslike townhouse office at Temple Place in London, Cliveden in what was then Buckinghamshire, Hever Castle in Kent, Villa Sirena in Sorrento. His largest single purchase, an entire balustrade from the Villa Borghese garden, including statues and fountain, he bought while serving as American minister in Rome and kept in storage until 1893, when he acquired the estate of Cliveden from the Duke of Westminster. In purchases ranging in size from coins to stately homes William Waldorf Astor may have been the grandest (as well as one of the most knowledgeable and scholarly) of the American grand acquisitors who gathered in the spoils of Europe in the late nineteenth century.

When President Arthur's term came to an end in 1885, Willy had to resign his post and return to New York. After his mother's death in 1887 and his father's in 1890, he assumed a senior position in the management of the Astor interests. He also resumed in earnest the old battle for social primacy with Caroline Astor, his cousin Jack's mother. Pride, primogeniture, and custodianship of the Astor family plate dictated, he believed, that his wife, Mamie, not the imperious Caroline, should be the publicly acknowledged head of the House of Astor. He urged Mamie to compete with her rival in the grandeur, frequency, and exclusiveness of her New York and Newport entertainments. Caroline Astor, however, was a much more formidable competitor in the social arena. She dismissed her nephew William as a nuisance, "a prickly sort of person," altogether unlike her adored and docile playboy son, John Jacob IV, and had as little to do with him as possible, which was agreeable to Willy. Caroline made a preemptive strike in her campaign for primacy by changing the wording on her calling card from "Mrs. William Astor" to "Mrs. Astor." She thereby relegated Willy's wife to second place and launched what amused observers on both sides of the Atlantic were soon calling "the Battle of the Cards." While the battle raged, it almost seemed that not since the Middle Ages, when rival popes at Rome and Avignon divided the Roman Catholic Church, had an issue of legitimacy stirred up such a *tzimmes*. Willy's gentle-natured wife did not have the stomach for battle. She was relieved when, following his "English Plan," he finally left Caroline in sole possession of her title and moved his family to London.

"America is not a fit place for a gentleman to live," Willy

announced to his former countrymen. "America is good enough for any man who has to make a livelihood, though why traveled people of independent means should remain there more than a week is not readily to be comprehended." Having "washed his hands of America and American methods," he was determined "no longer to be connected in any way with that country." William's aggressively insulting departure from New York provoked, among other send-offs from the press, a reference to the Astor family origins in "a German slaughterhouse" and the suggestion that the Astor coat of arms should be "a skunk, rampant, on a brindle ox-hide." Papers in the States reported that "William the Traitor" had been burned in effigy in the streets and likened to Benedict Arnold. William kept a scrapbook of these stories and often brooded over the abuse he suffered in the press.

In all likelihood it was Astor himself, out of the same perversity that prompted his farewell message to his countrymen, who was eventually responsible for inventing or approving a story blazoned across the front page of the *New York Times* on July 12, 1892. It was headlined: DEATH OF W. W. ASTOR. HE SUDDENLY EXPIRED YESTERDAY IN LONDON. By swallowing whole what later appeared to have been a hoax, the *Times* and other American newspapers had demonstrated what Willy saw as their habitual irresponsibility, slovenliness, and, above all, hypocrisy. For now, in an obituary of several thousand words, the *Times* extolled the former "William the Traitor" as "an ideal American," "a millionaire who believed in the American idea of government" and had done noble public service as legislator and diplomat:

> William Waldorf Astor was of all the Astors the one that
> was the most in touch with the great mass of the American

people. He was an ideal American, and for a man who was brought up in an aristocratic atmosphere and in constant contact with those who would be glad, perhaps, to see a plutocracy here, he was very much of a democrat. He believed thoroughly in the American idea of government and was the only one of his family that was ever active in politics, for which he had a commendable fondness. His services to his State and his party, while they were not long continued, were such as to be a credit to him.

The *Philadelphia Public Ledger* was equally unstinting and imaginative. "His nature was kindly, his manner simple, unaffected, sincere. He had many friends who admired him for his learning, his talents, and the noble qualities of heart which were his most distinguished characteristics." While accepting the story of his death as true, the *New York Tribune* said it was "not an event of great and lasting significance whether in the world of action or the world of thought."

The *Times* conceded that there had been "some curiously conflicting reports" as to the authenticity of the news. Like other doings and undoings of the very rich, the news of the death of William Waldorf Astor made too good a story to be allowed to succumb to checking.

MR. ASTOR NOT DEAD, the *Times* announced the next day, July 13. REPORTED AS RAPIDLY RECOVERING. Mr. Astor apparently enjoyed his obituaries and the gorgeous fantasy, familiar to him from his reading of *Tom Sawyer*, of observing mourners at his funeral and listening to his own funeral sermon. He "treated the affair with levity," according to a spokesman, and said he was getting used to being made a ghost. Normally he would not have tolerated a prank at his expense but would have dispatched a whole posse of lawyers to pursue the offender. But this prank was grand, transatlantic, and imperial, on a scale with Astor's ego and his fortune, and its eventual butt was not Astor but his old enemy, the American press. A threatened investigation of the hoax by British cable authorities trailed off into unsubstantiated published rumors that Astor had been mildly deranged at the time of his death notice. Perhaps, it was also rumored, he had absorbed the mystical teachings of Madame Helena Blavatsky, the late Russian soothsayer and conduit to the spirit world.

His public career behind him, and an immense fortune at his command, William was now freer than ever to indulge his passion for collecting, the arts, and a literary career. He founded a monthly publication, the *Pall Mall Magazine,* partly as an outlet for his short stories and his views on literature, history, politics, and American society. Rudyard Kipling, George Meredith, Algernon Charles Swinburne, Israel Zangwill, and Thomas Hardy were among the distinguished authors of the day who contributed fiction or verse to the magazine.

Several of Astor's own pieces in the magazine turned out to be its chief weak points and aroused both consternation and hilarity in his readers. As if inaugurating a brand-new line of inquiry, he entered the debate over the authorship of the works of William Shakespeare. "Even the staunchest adherents of the Stratford man admit the existence of a few awkward facts which cannot be explained away," Astor wrote. "Let us glance, briefly, at some of them." The historical Shakespeare, a butcher's son (like old John Jacob Astor), a sometime stage carpenter and actor, had terrible handwriting: "Fancy a play traced in such barbarous characters!"

"He was reputed intemperate; he was whipped for poaching; he married Anne Hathaway under circumstances discreditable to them both. At sixteen he is said to have been apprenticed to a butcher, after which he becomes a dealer in wood." This thoroughly inadequate creature spent the last decade of his life, Astor wrote, in a "dirty and soulless little village," and he died of a fever resulting from a drinking bout "of exceptional length and severity." "Is this," William concluded with a triumphant flourish, invoking the examples of Columbus, Napoleon, Luther, Newton, Galileo, Goethe, Richelieu, and Dante, "consistent with a great man's nature?" Astor's article became "a universal target for chaffing and ridicule," the *New York Times* correspondent, the novelist Harold Frederic, reported from London. "The second syllable of his name is clearly superfluous."

Following another line of scholarly inquiry, Astor tried to plumb the secret of the witty and beautiful Madame Juliette Recamier, object of the emperor Napoleon's "amorous advances," and concluded she had been married to her own father. In another much-quoted article he described London's famous fog, the city's chronic pall of mist and greasy coal smoke, as "an enveloping goddess in operatic raiment." He was unswayed by ridicule.

iii.

THE SENIOR, more thoughtful and brooding of the two Astor cousins, William Waldorf appointed himself family historian and defender. "I am glad my Great Grandfather was a successful trader," he wrote in his sixties, "because in all ages Trade has led the way to Civilization. I have studied his life, seeking to learn its aims, grateful to him for having lifted us above the ploughshares of Baden and bent on continuing his purpose." One result of these studies was a tén-thousand-word essay in which he reviewed his ancestor's allegedly maligned career and posthumous reputation. Willy concluded that the offending party in this systematic libel had been American democracy itself. Originally "the poor man's country," the United States had been undermined and betrayed in national purpose by envy, resentment, and a misguided hatred of wealth, distinction, and achievement. His great-grandfather's "life and character," Willy wrote, "have been distorted and caricatured until only an odd travesty survives. He has been continually derided and reviled with that spirit of pure malignity which pursued the successful man. It is not democratic to climb so high." Contrary to Willy, during the 1890s, and probably at any other time as well, so far from reviling and deriding rich people, the American public could hardly get enough of them—except, of course, for a few people who might be described by guardians of the social order as malcontents, radicals, and other ideological levelers embittered by envy and their own inadequacy. According to Mark Twain, the appetite for news of the moneyed classes and their doings could be satisfied even by a page-one headline RICH WOMAN FALLS DOWN STAIRS, NOT HURT.

Willy believed that it was the American press that led the vendetta against old John Jacob Astor. Journalists and popular biographers like James Parton deliberately transformed a man of "patient courage and masterful resolve: of forethought and suggestiveness and common sense" into an ogre about whom practically anything to his discredit could be believed.

In 1896, nearly half a century after old Astor's death, a Chicago lawyer named Franklin H. Head invented and put into circulation a brilliantly elaborated hoax. According to lawyer Head's compelling story, the source of John Jacob Astor's fortune, the acorn of his oak forest, was a rusty iron box, bearing on its lid the chiseled initials "W.K." and long buried in a cave on an island in Penobscot Bay, Maine. The box supposedly contained the fabled treasure that the British pirate Captain William Kidd had squirreled away against his old age. In 1701, before he was able to retire from piracy and enjoy his wealth, Kidd's countrymen hanged him, but not before he managed to leave Mrs. Kidd a cryptic note giving the location of his treasure chest. The search for this Monte Cristo trove of gold and jewels had been teasing the public imagination ever since Kidd's fateful date with the hangman. It drove the plots of Edgar Allan Poe's "The Gold Bug," Robert Louis Stevenson's *Treasure Island,* and now lawyer Head's almost thoroughly credible tale.

Old Astor was said to have acquired the box in a characteristically underhanded way through one of his French Canadian trappers. Until then, according to Head's review of the bank records, Astor had been "simply a modest trader, earning each year by frugality and thrift two or three hundred dollars above his living expenses, with a fair prospect of accumulating, by an industrious life, a fortune of twenty or thirty thousand dollars." But his acquisition of the box and subsequent sale of its contents to a London dealer in coins and precious stones coincided with a jump of about $1.3 million in his account, $700,000 of which he used to buy property in the city of New York.

Head's readers learned that in 1699 Winnepesaukee, head sachem of the Penobscot tribe, had deeded the island to Cotton Mather Olmsted, an Indian trader and ancestor of the distinguished landscape architect Frederick Law Olmsted, co-designer of Central Park. The place had remained in the family ever since.

Frederick Law Olmsted, its eventual heir and a close friend of Head's, allegedly sued the Astor estate for $5 million (the original $1.3 million plus accrued interest). Having been refused, he then demanded all the property in New York that John Jacob Astor, in effect a receiver of stolen goods, had purchased with the valuables Captain Kidd had taken from his victims and that more or less rightfully belonged to the Olmsteds. So much for the fruits of what William Waldorf Astor had memorialized as "patient courage and masterful resolve." The hoax was so credible, especially since it was reinforced by the long-standing Astor reputation for rapacity, that until he died in 1903, Olmsted repeatedly denied he had pursued a claim on the estate.

"None knew better how to make the utmost of opportunity," William wrote at the end of his long essay about his great-grandfather. "In the midst of indefatigable industry, a vein of sentimental sadness, of which his private papers give repeated indication, tinged his thoughts with a strange and retrospective pathos. Perhaps this was but a trace of the reverie of one who, grown meditative as the shadows lengthen, and passing the joys and loves and triumphs of a lifetime in review, catches beneath a thousand memories their inevitable undertone of tears." Old Astor had long continued to grieve over the death of his wife. John Jacob Astor II, their first son, was feebleminded, an imbecile in the terminology of the time, "a confirmed lunatic," according to Whitman. Three other Astor children had died in infancy.

Even after detailing such humanizing events William was not satisfied with his attempt to reconcile greatness, fame, and wealth with his ancestor's "peasant" origins and his "forlorn boyhood" spent in the "humble surroundings" of the family butcher shop.

Some vital, infusing element was missing from the Astor story, some aristocratic spark and genetic link that would account for what was perhaps a uniquely American phenomenon: John Jacob Astor, "a poor German lad . . . born in a peasant's cottage," had "sprung fresh from the people," as William wrote, but his heirs only one or two generations later were blue bloods bestriding the summit of the social heap. From an unimaginable height they looked down on "the people"—that is, if they were even aware that the people existed except to serve them and yield up tribute in rents. So they must have been blue bloods all along.

During the 1880s, while serving as U.S. minister to Italy, William had hired a firm of London genealogists—Janson, Cobb, Pearson and Company—to mouse around in French, German, and Spanish villages and search local histories and parish records for the name "Astor." Their five years of expensive digging dead-ended in a Baden butcher shop owned by "Jacob Ashdor," father of John Jacob Astor. The genealogists had better luck, William believed, in tracking a somewhat similar name, "d'Astorga," that belonged to a dynasty going back to Count Pedro d'Astorga of Castille, a Crusader killed at the siege of Jerusalem in 1100 while locked in mortal combat with the Saracen "Yusuf Tashafin, King of the Almoravids of Morocco." Some years earlier, the researchers reported, an unnamed "Spanish Queen" had granted to one of Pedro's ancestors "the arms of a Falcon, Argent, on a gloved hand, Or, in acknowledgment of the recapture of her favorite Falcon. The recipient adopted as his name the Spanish word Azor (The Goshawk)." Among more recent Astor forebears, according to this account, was "Jean Jacques d'Astorg," a French Huguenot of noble descent who had fled to Germany "upon the Revocation of the Edict of Nantes in 1685" and died near Heidelberg in 1711. Some twenty generations of blood allegedly linked John Jacob Astor of Waldorf, who died in New York in 1848, with the Christian warrior who died in Jerusalem in 1100.

In a devastating article in the *New York Sun,* Lothrop Withington, dean of American genealogists, pronounced the Astor tree pure moonshine, a "fabrication" riddled with inaccuracies and phoney dates. A real-life Comte d'Astorga living in France dismissed it as "an appalling mixture of facts, some of them actually turned upside down." No evidence whatsoever supported any connection between the Spanish Crusader who fell at Jerusalem and a clan of beer-swilling, hog-butchering Germans in the village of Waldorf, duchy of Baden. There was, however, the remote but mortifying possibility, as Withington pointed out, that the putative founder of the Astor dynasty, if one could be found, had not been a Crusader but a Jewish doctor of Carcassonne named Isaac Astorg, who died in 1305.* William's London researchers warned him that the Astorga/Astor connection was at best an exercise in the optative mood. But he was so pleased with this genealogy that, dismissing all doubts and objections, he reproduced it as a full-page illustration in his great-grandfather's biography.

In point of authenticity, the Astorga/Astor connection scarcely differed from other fanciful lineages that American plutocrats were buying by the yard, along with needy dukes and lords as mates for their daughters. Referring to William as "an eminent semi-American," a *New York Times* editorial said, "Everybody knew before that 'family trees' were delicate vegetables, soon to be

---

*A member of the high-toned Cabot family of Boston had also met up with a Jewish trip wire in the genealogical underbrush. His hired researcher, soon after abruptly dismissed, had traced the Cabot origins back to some tenth-century Lombardy Jews. (See Leon Harris, *Only to God* [New York, 1967], 4.)

shaken to pieces by the wind of investigation." As always William refused to be shaken by either ridicule or revelation. His Spanish Crusader was the central actor in his version of what Sigmund Freud was to call "family romances," daydreams about replacing forebears with "others of better birth. The technique used in carrying out phantasies like this . . . depends upon the ingenuity and the material which the child has at his disposal." The adult William had plenty of both. When he became a British subject in 1899 he adopted a personal coat of arms, a silver goshawk perched on a gold-gloved hand. He displayed it along with shields, banners, and other heraldic furnishings at Cliveden, his great estate in the Thames Valley, and at Hever Castle, his moated retreat in the Kent countryside.

Eventually, reflecting on what he claimed was the implacable American resentment of Astor greatness, William gave up, at least privately, the battle to claim a noble ancestry. "I do not believe," he wrote to an American friend, Amy Small Richardson, in 1905, "that anything would avail to change the ordinary acceptation in America of my great-grandfather's life and character. He will go down as a 'Dutch sausage peddler,' and my fate promises to be the same if the American press can make it so." He consoled himself with the hope of one day being elevated to the British peerage.

THREE

Inventor and Novelist

i.

FROM CHILDHOOD John Jacob Astor IV was an unlikely counterpart to his powerful older cousin, William Waldorf Astor. Pampered by his mother and his four older sisters, neglected by a distant, dissipated, and frequently absent father, he was socially and physically graceless. A long beanpole body and relatively small head made him look as if he had been assembled from mismatched parts. He seemed dreamy and affectless, someone almost to be pitied despite his wealth, position, and flashes of seigneurial authority. A lonely and awkward adolescent, he was sent away to prep school at St. Paul's, in Concord, New Hampshire, after which he spent three years at Harvard as a special student. He enrolled in science courses and left without taking a degree. After a year or two of travel in Europe, India, and Egypt, in 1887, at the age of twenty-three, he returned to New York to take his place as scion of the cadet branch of the Astors. Like a debutante, he was formally introduced to society at an eight-hundred-guest reception his mother, Caroline Webster Schermerhorn Astor, gave in his honor at her house on Fifth Avenue at Thirty-fourth Street. The scandal sheet *Town Topics* hailed young Astor on his entrance into the mating market as "one of the richest catches of the day," and added,

"It is very questionable whether, were he put to it, he could ever earn his bread by his brains." He was not put to it to any extent until after his father died five years later and left him, at least nominally, in charge of a staff of lawyers, accountants, and managers who, along with several trustees, were responsible for administering his share of the Astor estate.

Soon after his debut, Jack got into a much-publicized brawl with another young blade of blue-blood extraction, Beekman Kip Burrowe, in the men's room at fashionable Sherry's Restaurant. They quarreled over which of them should have the privilege of sitting with a young upper-class beauty they both fancied. The two gentlemen went at each other with fists and walking sticks before someone separated them. "It's been a long time," a newspaper commented, "since any incident has occasioned so much amusement in society." In consequence the press awarded Jack Astor the inevitable punning nickname that was to follow him most of the days of his life, "Jack Ass."

Caroline Astor's son had a reputation for making clumsy and urgent advances to the wives, sisters, and daughters of his social class and for getting himself into other sorts of scrapes. To serve the white marble double house he later built for himself and his mother on upper Fifth Avenue, he announced his intention to put up a two-story stable for their horses and carriages. The proposed site for the stable was a twenty-five-by-one-hundred-foot lot he owned around the corner on Madison Avenue and Sixty-fifth Street. If built there, his stable would have abutted B'Nai Jeshurun, the city's largest Orthodox synagogue. Synagogue officers and the neighbors, non-Jews as well as Jews, were outraged. "We condemn the spirit of Mr. Astor in disregarding our desires, interests, and rights in the premises, and we denounce his threatened act as unbecoming a landowner of this city, to which he is so greatly indebted." Jack and the managers of the Astor estate refused the offer of the synagogue trustees to buy the lot from him for $61,000. According to a spokesman at the estate office, "Mr. Astor needs another stable, and he is going to build it there." The protesters drew up a formal resolution listing their grievances and submitted a bill (subsequently vetoed by the governor) forbidding "the housing of animals . . . within 100 feet of a house of worship." After six months of acrimonious debate—and playful editorial discussions of fleas, stable odors, stable noises, and equine hygiene in general—Jack withdrew his plan, but not before leaving an indelible impression of contemptuous behavior.

With such a reputation, anything even conventionally laudable that he did was bound to attract surprise and comment. JOHN JACOB ASTOR A JUROR, the *New York Times* reported in a page-one story. He had answered the summons and presented himself for jury duty, it was noted, instead of buying his way out by paying a fine, like other "millionaires of prominence," among them polo enthusiast George Gould. Astor gave his business as "real estate" and served attentively on a case involving a shipment of eggs. He then had himself excused from further service on the grounds of having a prior engagement.

At about the same time (November 1893) as the stable-synagogue dustup, Jack inserted himself in the case of a drifter named John Garvin, an unemployed former grocery clerk and worker in a Bowery shooting gallery. A laundress in the Astor mansion had returned from a night out to find Garvin naked and sound asleep in her bed, with his hat, coat, shirt, and trousers piled on a chair. How Garvin got into the Astor house in the first place no one knew for sure, not even Garvin. He clearly "had a few pin wheels in his head," according to Mrs. Astor's English butler, and may have suffered a brain injury from a rifle-loading accident at his Bowery job. A judge at the Jefferson Market Police Court fined Garvin $5 for disorderly conduct and released him after a benevolent stranger paid the fine. "I am utterly at a loss," Jack said, "to understand why anyone should want to pay the fellow's fine and let him get away, and I think it is a most outrageous act. . . . It does not seem to me right that a man can enter the house of a citizen and be fined only $5," Jack went on. "A great piece of injustice has been done." He put himself forward as protector of the public welfare as well as the Astor property. "My mother is naturally alarmed by her experience and something must be done to punish Garvin, so that he will not attempt to repeat his offense. If he goes free, hundreds of persons may imitate his example. . . . Such a state of things is not to be tolerated, and I do not propose that it shall be." On Jack's insistence, Garvin was immediately rearrested, charged with attempted burglary, locked up, and held on $1,000 bail.

Soon famous as the tramp who slept in one of Mrs. Astor's beds, even celebrated in a popular song, Garvin became a sort of public pet, a victim, as it appeared, of double jeopardy, false arrest, and the privileged wrath of a rich man who had appointed himself a champion of justice and appeared to have lost any sense of proportion. At the expense of his admirers, for about six months Garvin enjoyed cigars and steak-and-egg dinners with extra bread in his cell in the Tombs. He was finally carted off to the State Asylum for Insane Criminals at Matteawan.

Missteps aside, to his mother's immense gratification and relief, Jack entered into a diplomatically brilliant alliance that reinforced her own already secure standing as queen of American society. At twenty-six he married Ava Lowle Willing of Philadelphia, a great beauty of impeccable breeding and bloodlines. "It was not alone her beautiful face," said society eminence Mrs. J. Bordon Harriman, a respected authority on such matters, "but the *tout ensemble*, arms, wrists, hands, ankles, and a brilliant distinction that was unforgettable." "She rides well," the *Times* reported, "dances beautifully, is musical, quite literary and uncommonly intelligent." What was more, this spectacular specimen of American young womanhood came from a blood-proud and prominent family. Genealogists hired by the Philadelphia Willings had drawn up a family tree showing descent, on Ava's mother's side, from Alfred the Great and several other potentates, including Henry I of France and Henry IV of England. Their glittering history put the Willings several rungs above the Astors, whose not-so-distant patriarch, as they were often reminded, had come from the bottom.* Among the wedding gifts from the groom's parents were a furnished house on Fifth Avenue and diamonds from Caroline Astor's jewel case.

The same hand that assembled Jack apparently assembled the Astor-Willing marriage as well. It was even rumored that the bride had wept on the eve of her wedding and begged her parents to call it off. The day of the wedding private trains laid on by the

---

*After granting a rare interview, Caroline Astor instructed her maid to offer Nixola Greeley-Smith, a reporter for the *New York World*, a $2 tip for her trouble. The reporter was Horace Greeley's granddaughter, and she had a ready answer (much polished in the retelling). "Will you deliver a message exactly as I give it to you?" she said to the maid. "Tell Mrs. Astor she not only forgets who I am, but she forgets who she is. Give her back the two dollars with my compliments and tell her that when John Jacob Astor was skinning rabbits my grandfather was getting out the *Tribune* and was one of the foremost citizens of New York."

Pennsylvania Railroad carried the cream of New York society to a city by tradition unaccustomed to such bustle and splendor. The marriage proved to be a miserable affair almost from the moment in February 1891 that the couple exchanged vows in the parlor of the Willing town house on South Broad Street. Ava did her dynastic duty by producing a son, William Vincent, nine months after the wedding night. Then she turned her energies elsewhere. She devoted herself to tennis, skiing, bridge, and other fashionable amusements. Once the then-current mah-jongg fever infected her, she was to be seen in Chinese restaurants on Mott Street in Manhattan taking lessons from Oriental masters of the game. By all accounts, Ava was self-indulgent, extravagant, and sharp-tongued. But, especially in contrast to her husband, she was also spirited, untrammeled, charming, and distinctly unstuffy, not above stopping in for a beer at a neighborhood saloon. She persuaded Jack to commission a friend of theirs, the architect Stanford White, to build an athletic complex at Ferncliff, the Astor country estate near Rhinebeck: it comprised a tennis court, two squash courts, a marble swimming pool, a bowling alley, a billiard room, and a rifle range. Ava had no interest in her husband beyond his money, which paid for such expensive improvements, and she made no attempt to hide this, even abusing him in front of guests and the help.

Elizabeth Lehr, partner in a *mariage blanc* with Harry Lehr, one of Caroline Astor's pets, was often a guest at Ferncliff. She recalled that while Ava and her coterie played bridge, Jack "shambled from room to room, tall, loosely built, and ungraceful, rather like a great overgrown colt, in a vain search for someone to talk to." When he switched on one of the player pianos he had installed in the house, a footman informed him that Mrs. Astor complained the music was disturbing her bridge players and wanted it stopped. "And he would sigh and turn it off." Elizabeth went on:

> He was not particularly fond of music, but the mechanical system of the pianos interested him; it offered a temporary diversion at least. . . . He would go up to his room and dress faultlessly for dinner, come down, prepared to talk and enter-tain his guests, and find everyone scurrying upstairs to make hasty, last-minute toilets. Of course they would all be late, which annoyed him intensely, for he made a god of punctu-ality, and the probability of a spoiled dinner in consequence did not improve his temper, for he was a notable epicure. The house party would come down to find him, watch in hand, constrained and irritable.

Jack mostly remained silent at Ava's dinner table, where the conversation generally turned to postmortems of the afternoon's bridge games. On Sundays "he would come downstairs ready for church in cutaway coat and immaculate topper, only to find rub-bers in progress already. So he would sit alone in his front pew, come back to lunch off a tray in his study, and return to New York in the afternoon, a lonely man in spite of all his acquaintances."

Virtually a specter in his own houses, Jack spent much of his time away from Ava in the company of their son, Vincent (as he preferred to be called), who adored him and was adored in return. Ava called the boy stupid and avoided him because he was clumsy and lumpish looking, had big feet, and, perhaps worst of all, re-minded her of his father. Jack was happiest sailing with Vincent on board *Nourmahal,* the steel-hulled steam yacht he had inherited from his pleasure-loving father. In refitting the yacht he added, among other features, a dining saloon capable of sitting sixty people, a forty-two-foot steam launch, an electric launch, and a battery of rapid-firing guns. They were installed on deck in readiness to repel Caribbean and Barbary Coast pirates *Nourmahal* might encounter on her cruises. Newspapers dutifully reported mishaps on the water that shaped Jack's reputation as a lubberly yachtsman, although his hired captains and crews were mostly to blame. Over a period of only a few years the accident-prone *Nourmahal* ran aground in the Hudson, rammed the Vanderbilt yacht *North Star*, impaled herself on rocks off Newport, and collided with a ferry in New York Harbor. The yacht's electric launch, the *Corcyra*, built to Jack's design and specifications, sank after being run over by a steamer.

Ashore, Jack isolated himself in the laboratory he ordered built for himself at Ferncliff. From his lonely boyhood on, and especially after his science education at Harvard, he had been a passionate tinkerer and aspiring inventor. Electricity and speed fascinated him, as did machinery of all sorts, in particular motor cars: his garage contained as many as eighteen, some of them designed for racing. In Paris in 1903 he was to make an ascent in the personal flying machine invented by the Brazilian dandy Alberto Santos-Dumont. Jack was happy and confident at the throttle of an Illinois Central locomotive that he drove for six hours one day with as much panache, the papers reported, as if it had been one of his own fast cars. (In taking over the throttle of the locomotive, engineer Jack, living out the daydream of many American boys, exercised his authority as the railroad's major stockholder.) He invented or projected an improved bicycle brake; a "rain-inducer" that blew warm moist air up into the clouds (he never tried it, he said, "but it would probably work"); a "pneumatic road-improver"

that blasted away dust and dried horse manure from paved surfaces (it won a prize at the Chicago Exposition in 1893); a suction-
cup system mounted on the legs of deck chairs and other steamer
furniture to keep them from sliding in heavy weather; and an improved marine turbine engine. In its May 1909 issue *Scientific
American* reported that Astor was constructing at Ferncliff a plant
to compress and convert deposits of peat into a gas usable as a fuel
for vehicles and machines. "The patent application is now pending
and on its being allowed Colonel Astor intends to present it to the
public." He pasted in his scrapbook about two dozen news clips
on the subject from the *Times* and papers across the country, all of
them promising a bright future of cheap fuel. Two of the headlines
were PEAT GAS ERA MAY BE NEAR and EVERY FARM MAY NOW PRODUCE
GAS. The device probably required too much energy in processing
the raw material to make the end product worthwhile.

"In the evolved city of the future," Jack had written in a letter
in *Scientific American,* "street pavements will of course be smooth
and easily cleaned—asphalt, bitumen, macadam, or sheet steel; and
to keep horses in large cities will doubtless be prohibited by the
Board of Health, as stabling cows, pigs, or sheep is now. Second-
story sidewalks composed largely of translucent glass, leaving all
the present street level to vehicles, are already badly needed . . .
and will doubtless have made their appearance in less than twenty
years."

Peace reigned in Jack's world of the future. "As zoology shows
us," he wrote, "the amphibian metamorphosed into the land verte-
brate, followed by the bird, so history reveals the aborigine's
dugout, the Fifth Avenue omnibus, and the oxcart, followed by
the automobile which is preparing the light and powerful engine
that will soon propel the flying machine. That will be a happy day

for earth-dwellers, for war will become so destructive that it will probably bring its own end; and the human caterpillar, already mechanically converted into the grasshopper, will become a fairly beautiful butterfly." "Next to religion," Jack believed, "we have most to hope from science."

Chronically humorless, he was not given to practical joking, although practical joking, instead of an unquestioning eagerness to believe, would have been the only charitable explanation for a signed article Jack published in William Randolph Hearst's daily *New York American*. He recounted a remarkable discovery. "While automobiling in the Pyrenees mountains a few years ago, [I] observed an unusual creature. It had a shaggy coat, thick legs, and a slouching gait. It belonged to some gypsies who had a number of dogs and a performing bear, and they described it as a bear-dog." Astor bought the animal, which he found to be "intellectually and physically far superior to an ordinary dog," and took it back with him to Ferncliff, where he kept it along with his pedigreed sheep and other prized livestock. He cited his bear-dog as proof of a long-standing belief of his that animals of different genera could together produce a creature that was neither one nor the other but at least theoretically more valuable and useful than either.

According to Dr. William Hornaday, director of the Bronx Zoological Garden, Astor's bear-dog was probably just a dwarf St. Bernard that the Gypsies had put over on this rich innocent. He suggested that Astor apply his mind to genetic engineering and animal husbandry. He might make a second Astor fortune, Hornaday said, "if he could invent an animal to eat dirt, for dirt is very cheap."

SCIENTISTS SCOFF AT ASTOR'S BEAR-DOG, the *Times* headlined its two-column story. BRONX ZOO DIRECTOR THINKS [ASTOR] OUGHT TO

OFFER A PRIZE FOR A REAL LIVE MASTODON. In his article in the *American,* Astor cited laboratory experiments with frogs' eggs conducted by a Professor Albert Oppel of the University of Halle, in Germany. Professor Oppel had apparently succeeded in breeding a frog two feet high. Astor saw no reason other creatures could not be similarly enlarged by selective breeding. It might even be possible to bring back extinct giant creatures of the Carboniferous period; use them both as farm animals, like oxen and draft horses, and as a meat source for humans; and, meanwhile, feed them cheaply. His nutritional logic appeared to be impeccable. "While our coal was being formed," he explained, "vegetation as we know it probably did not exist. Since the mammoths and their contemporaries must have eaten the plants that became coal, why may not their descendants eat some preparation of peat, coal, crude oil, or even limestone when the progress of the world requires that they should?" Astor was "so deeply interested," the *Times* reported, "that he has offered a prize of $5000 for the best bear-dog to be entered at next year's dog show at Madison Square Garden."

In 1894 Jack had followed cousin Willy's ventures into novel writing with a work of science fiction, *A Journey in Other Worlds: A Romance of the Future,* published by D. Appleton and Company. The illustrations were by Dan Beard, who had done the pictures for Mark Twain's *A Connecticut Yankee at King Arthur's Court.* His work for Jack's novel showed, among other wonders, an ascent by flying machine from Van Cortlandt Park in the Bronx; a race with a comet; space travel to Jupiter, Mars, and Saturn; and encounters there with mastodonic animals and the souls of the righteous dead. Jack's tale, inspired by Jules Verne, was set in the year 2000, by which time Manhattan dwellers, presumably kept in check by the Republican Party, the Episcopal Church, and a terror of socialism and anarchism, enjoyed many blessings of science and technology: the "kintograph"—"a visual telegraph"—that put scientists in New York in visual contact with engineers and workmen on the shores of Baffin Bay; fast electric automobiles; a convenient subway system; and an existence made want free through the harnessing of a force Jack called "Apergy." Apergy combined "negative and positive electricity with electricity of the third element or state." Elijah, Jesus, and other ancients had at least suspected the existence of this miraculous force.

In Jack's world of the future, scientists employed by the Terrestrial Axis Straightening Company harnessed apergy to nullify gravity, melt the polar ice cap, and blow up the Aleutian Islands. All this had been done in order "to straighten the axis of the earth, to combine the extreme heat of summer with the intense cold of winter and produce a uniform temperature for each degree of latitude the year round." By the year 2000, according to Jack's prediction, the United States would have absorbed not only Canada but Mexico, Central America, and parts of South America as well. The banana republics south of the border with Mexico would have finally tired of "incessant revolutions" and turned for protection and stability to the governance of the Great White Father in Washington. And, just as old John Jacob Astor had known in his bones, Manhattan Island had continued to thrive. By 2000, according to Jack's projection, it had a population of 2.5 million and was surrounded by Greater New York's population belt of an additional 12 million. Comic stumbles aside, Jack's free-ranging imagination looked ahead to television, global warming, and genetic engineering and was not without predictive value for someone whose family business was real estate.

FOUR

Palaces for the People

i.

W RITING IN 1884, E. L. Godkin, editor and founder of the *Nation,* recalled that American hotels had long been among the wonders of the New World. Impressed by their size and lavishness, some travelers from abroad came near to assuming that the natives lived in hotels and that "home life in a house was almost unknown on this side of the Atlantic." Putting up such hotels, and becoming, in effect, innkeepers, was far from maverick behavior for John Jacob Astor's breed of American capitalist and for his great-grandsons three generations later.

A Scots newspaper editor named John Leng, visiting the United States in 1876, the centennial of the Republic, noted what he called "a peculiar propensity," not found among Europeans, "of men who have become rich in the States to build hotels" on a scale that reflected "the largeness of American ideas" and of the North American continent. Looking back, Leng cited the founding Astor along with Astor's near contemporary, New York merchant prince Alexander Turney Stewart. Along with the world's largest dry-goods store, a five-story "iron palace" (as it was called) that displayed acres of quality goods, and the marble mansion on Fifth Avenue where he lived, Stewart built and owned two hotels: the opulent Metropolitan on lower Broadway and the Grand Union, at Saratoga Springs, a fashionable health resort and horse-racing center in upstate New York. San Francisco real estate tycoon James Lick put up a fancy hotel at the corner of Montgomery and Sutter streets, named it after himself, and lived there until he died in 1876. Lick House's restaurant, where Mark Twain and other local celebrities dined on oysters, buffalo steak, and champagne, copied the banquet hall in the palace of Versailles.

Another San Francisco mogul, William Chapman Ralston, founder and president of the Bank of California, the dominant financial institution of the Far West, opened his gigantic Palace Hotel in 1875. Built to be earthquakeproof and enclosed within three-foot-thick brick walls girdled with iron bands, "the Greatest Caravansary in the World," as a local newspaper described it, occupied an entire city block—over two acres—and stood seven stories high over Market and Montgomery streets. Among other wonders, Ralston's Palace offered "Promenades Amidst Tropical Verdure," innovative water closets that functioned "without producing the horrid noise one usually hears," and "Electric Bells Everywhere" that required 125 miles of wiring. A run on his bank together with the deficit financing of his no-expense-spared hotel left Ralston several million dollars in debt. Possibly a suicide, he was last seen alive swimming off North Beach in the direction of Alcatraz Island.

Put up in 1892 by wealthy businessman and real-estate promoter Henry Cordis Brown, the Palace Hotel in Denver had a seven-story balconied lobby with a stained-glass ceiling, served food from its own outlying farms and dairies, and briefly offered a crematorium for guests who had made their last stop on earth at the hotel. Brown's Palace was almost as famous, although still not nearly so grand as merchant prince Potter Palmer's hotel in Chicago. An earlier Palmer House, although advertised as "the only fireproof hotel in the world," had been one of the first buildings to go in the great fire of 1871. Palmer replaced it immediately with a larger and more ambitious place. At eight stories, it was the city's tallest building and occupied an entire block along State Street. Palmer made the hotel his wedding gift to his highborn and cultivated wife, Bertha Honoré of Louisville, famous for her Paris couture and her trademark item of personal adornment, a seven-strand necklace of 2,268 pearls.

The most lavishly decorated and upholstered establishment of its kind, Palmer House was quickly known the world over for its liveried staff and sixty-foot bar. Its marble-pillared lobby-arcade served as informal stock and commodities exchange, news center, and public clubhouse. In the basement was a magnificent "tonsorial parlor" which the lessee decorated with 225 silver dollars set in a checkerboard pattern on its tiled floor. An immediate sensation, Palmer House's barbershop floor was soon copied all over the country. The epidemic of "Silver Dollar Saloons" extended to a gangster hangout on New York's Lower East Side that outdid Palmer House: in the floor were 1,000 silver dollars, while an additional 500 glittered in the gaslit chandeliers.

Palmer House was "a gilded and mirrored rabbit-warren," according to Rudyard Kipling. "A Hottentot would not have been guilty of this sort of barbarism." The lobby was "crammed with people talking about money, and spitting about everywhere," he wrote. "Other barbarians charged in and out of this inferno with letters and telegrams in their hands, and yet others shouted at each other. A man who had drunk quite as much as was good for him told me that this was 'the finest hotel in the finest city on God

Almighty's earth.' " At a Sunday service in a nearby church Kipling listened to a sermon "delivered with a voice of silver and with imagery borrowed from the auction-room." The minister offered congregants the vision of "a heaven on the lines of the Palmer House (but with all the gilding real gold and all the plate-glass diamond)."

Although busy with more profitable and extensive ventures in Chicago real estate, Palmer supervised every detail of the building and furnishing of his hotel. After it opened for business he kept in touch with daily operations from a little windowed office looking into the main lobby. For all the gaudiness and bustle of the place, Palmer saw to it that at least upstairs it had some of the character of a refined private house. No such private house, however, presented guests with an illustrated room-service menu that showed, on one side, a pigsty and hovel, symbolic of "Chicago forty years ago," and, on the other, an idealized image of "The Chicago of To-day!" In addition to gargantuan beefsteaks and roasts of bear, antelope, and mountain sheep, the menu offered delicate fare like boned quail, blackbird, and partridge, and fairyland confections of spun sugar and fruit ices. Palmer, his wife, and their two sons, both born on the premises, lived in the hotel. He called it "my house," "my home." Bertha, the Mrs. Astor of the Midwest, maintained a dignified silence when a guest of honor at Palmer House, the infanta Eulalia, representing the king and queen of Spain at Chicago's Columbian Exposition in 1893, snubbed her because she was "an innkeeper's wife." According to her biographer, Ishbel Ross, Bertha maintained her composure and said she "had no objection to being called the innkeeper's wife. She was quite fond of the innkeeper."

Rockefeller partner and secretary-treasurer of the Standard Oil

Company, by the 1880s Henry M. Flagler was one of the richest men in the country. A former freight handler on the Erie Canal and part owner of a whiskey distillery, after making his pile in petroleum with Standard Oil, he entered a second youth as a builder of hotels and rail lines along Florida's east coast. He transformed the area's desolate beaches and steamy alligator-infested wilderness into a winter playground for the rich. Moving like Sherman's army on its March to the Sea, Flagler's construction battalions swept south from Jacksonville and St. Augustine. "He seemed but to wave his magic wand," Colonel William D'Alton Mann's book of vanity biographies, *Representative Americans,* said about Flagler, "and there arose out of the earth a palatial caravansary which for architectural beauty and magnificence has never been equaled in any land." Flagler's "discovery" of Florida proved to be more consequential than Ponce de León's four centuries earlier. He took a hands-on as well as a close supervisory interest in his hotels, sometimes pitching in to speed up construction and, on at least one occasion, slashing furniture upholstery to check on the springs and stuffing underneath. According to local legend, when his Royal Poinciana was finished, Flagler decided to upgrade the social landscape by ousting the surrounding community (known as the "Styx") of black construction workers. He declared a holiday, sent the workers and their families off to attend a circus as his guests, and, while they were gone, burned down their tents and shacks. He resettled his workers in West Palm Beach.

Among the reverses Flagler met up with in his otherwise unimpeded progress as innkeeper was his failure—the cause of a permanent estrangement—to transmit his passion for hotels to his son Harry. Harry cared about music, not business, and after two years of forced apprenticeship in Florida fled to New York and became a patron of the Philharmonic. Meanwhile, Ida Alice, Flagler's second wife, had conceived a passion for Czar Nicholas II, Autocrat of All the Russias, and claimed to be communicating with him by means of her Ouija board. She believed that the czar returned her love and they would marry as soon as Henry died, assuming she managed to survive attempts by Henry and their family doctor to poison her. In 1897 Alice was put away for good in a sanitarium in Pleasantville, New York. She told her keepers she was of royal blood, born Princess Ida Alice von Schotten Tech. Applying cash and clout, in 1901 Flagler levered the Florida state legislature into passing a general law (known to the tabloid-reading public as the "Flagler Divorce Law" and soon repealed) that made four years of insanity grounds for divorce. Seven days after the divorce went through, Flagler, seventy-one, announced his engagement to his long-standing companion, thirty-four-year-old Mary Lily Kenan. His wedding gift to her was a $2.5 million marble mansion, "Whitehall," commissioned from the firm of John Carrere and Thomas Hastings, architects of Flagler's first hotel in St. Augustine (and, later, of the monumental New York Public Library building on Fifth Avenue, opened in 1911).

From their glowing palace the happy couple ruled over Palm Beach, the town Flagler had created and made into an American Riviera. "This is an amazing winter resort," Henry James wrote from his rooms at the Breakers, "the well-to-do in their tens, their hundreds of thousands, from all over the land, the property of a single enlightened despot, the creator of two monster hotels. . . . It will give me brilliant chapters on hotel-civilization." When this seigneurial innkeeper, Henry Flagler, died in 1913, his widow had his body embalmed and transported over the rail lines his battalions had built, from Palm Beach to St. Augustine. There he lay in state, his own guest of honor, in the lobby of the Ponce de Leon, his first Florida hotel.

Luxury aside, one feature common to these showplaces and civic ornaments was that they had been planned and built by men at the top of the social and financial heap and proud to be innkeepers. Not without enjoying the enhancement of their personal grandeur, Flagler, Palmer, and the others created intricate artificial worlds that were self-contained and self-sustaining and aimed at achieving perfection in every detail. For all the bricks, marble, velvet, structural iron, and financial accounting that went into their construction, their grand hotels could even be called ventures in the ideal.

ii.

By the 1890s the Astor estate, comprising the assets of both cousins, was worth about $200 million. In the 1930s the historian Burton J. Hendrick called it "the world's greatest monument to unearned increment . . . a first mortgage on Fate itself." By extrapolation Hendrick figured the Astor holdings would be worth $80 billion by the year 2000. The Fifth Avenue block alone, where the two had grown up in their parents' adjacent houses, was valued at $35 million. This was about a thousand times what the founder's son, William Backhouse Sr., "landlord of New York," had paid for it half a century earlier when it was part of a farm. Along with their enormous fortune William Waldorf and John Jacob IV had inherited their great-grandfather's cast-iron certainty that the island of Manhattan, thirteen miles long and two at its broadest, was destined to be the capital of the New World and of the Old World as well.

Obeying the ancestral impulse that in the 1830s led the family founder to build Astor House, the grandest American hotel of its time, William Waldorf Astor, too, became a builder of hotels on a grand scale. He commissioned the towering steel-framed New Netherland (the original name of the Dutch settlement in North America) on Fifth Avenue at Fifty-ninth Street. He also bought a large parcel of property on Broadway, in the crossroads area soon to be named Times Square, where he would eventually build the Hotel Astor. But the most imperial and innovative of such ventures of his was one that would revolutionize both hotel keeping on the North American continent and the social rhythms of New York City.

William was to name it the Waldorf, as much in honor of himself as of old John Jacob Astor's hometown in Baden. His choice of a site for the Waldorf, Fifth Avenue and Thirty-third Street, was equally freighted with a sense of history but also motivated by feelings of oedipal succession, long-standing clan antagonism and rivalry, and undisguised vindictiveness. Both his mother and father had died by 1890–1891, when he ordered construction of the Waldorf. He tore down the house where they had lived for almost all of their married life, where he had been born in 1848, and where he had grown up in an atmosphere of solemn and unblemished probity. His aunt Caroline's redbrick-and-brownstone house next door, long the scene of her famous entertainments, was to be made virtually uninhabitable by the noise, dust, traffic, and general tumult of excavation and construction. Dwarfed and demeaned, her house and garden cowered in the shadow of William's immense building. To the south Caroline could see eleven stories of blank brick wall interrupted only by an open-sided air shaft.

Putting up the Waldorf where he did had been motivated by a punitive as well as an ego-serving purpose. It was a preemptive strike against Caroline and her son Jack, this time on a field of combat larger than a pasteboard calling card. The *Times* recognized that the prospect of this hotel rising where it did sparked "a variety of rumors," some of them hardly new, that indicated "something in the nature of a family feud between the two branches of the Astors." To accommodate his mother and his own family, Jack spent $2 million to build a four-story French Renaissance chateau uptown on Fifth Avenue and Sixty-fifth Street. The double house designed by the fashionable architect Richard Morris Hunt boasted the city's largest private ballroom.

Even before the cornerstone was laid, the *Times* had hailed the imminent arrival of Wllliam Waldorf Astor's "veritable palace," the most luxurious hotel in the United States. To somber and low-lying brownstone New York, Astor's Waldorf brought exuberant high-rise architecture, European glitter, elegance, and detailing. It was an expatriate's declaration of personal magnificence, blue-blood pride, and superiority in imagination, style, and intellect to the members of his class and the nation at large. He kept an eye on the layout and decoration of his hotel, stipulating, for example, hand-painted decorative ceilings in each room, bathrooms that opened out on a wide court, and such imported innovations as a concierge to preside over the hotel entrance and bestow at least a fleeting sense of electedness on those he admitted. One of the small private restaurants replicated the dining room of his parents' house, its furnishings intact and the table set for fourteen places with the Astor family service. When the building was done, William came to see it only once on a visit from London, and he walked quickly through the corridors. He stopped for no one and kept his eyes focused on the floor. This was in keeping with his personal style of aristocratic aloofness. He did not attend the opening in 1893.

To run the Waldorf he leased it to a man who was equally autocratic and had similar aspirations for a new and superior sort of establishment that would introduce Americans to "marvelous ways of living and luxuries hitherto unattainable." George C. Boldt, former proprietor of the successful Bellevue-Stratford in Philadelphia, was a natural-born public-relations master. Boldt knew where the social and money power lay, how to attract and massage it, how to transform an occasion into an event, and an event like the Waldorf's opening into an archetype of its kind. Obsequious or overbearing, as the circumstances demanded, he lavished wine, flowers, baskets of fruit, cigars, and special privileges on favored guests. He treated the less favored with a hauteur and an abruptness that established a stereotype for future hotel executives. He once tore up the bill of a guest who had the temerity to question some charges and then banished him from the premises forever. ("I fought with the management, over everything as with beasts at Ephesus," an English friend told Henry James after staying a day or two at the Waldorf. "It's an awful place, and my bill was the awfullest part of it.") For his Palm Garden restaurant, the most exclusive and expensive eating place in the city, he hired only waiters who could speak French and German. He wore a mustache and a beard, but he ordered his employees, and even the cab drivers lined up outside for fares, to shave theirs off. The order stuck, despite charges of infringed personal liberties from labor unions and the governor, a bearded man named Roswell Pettibone Flower. Boldt was a perfect surrogate for William Waldorf Astor.

Boldt launched his long career at the hotel in March 1893 with a spectacular concert evening for the benefit of St. Mary's Hospital for Children. To celebrate the Waldorf's official opening he recruited leaders of New York, Boston, Baltimore, and Philadelphia society to sponsor an event that drew about 1,500 select guests. The line of carriages delivering them extended along Fifth Avenue from Washington Square to Fifty-ninth Street. Once arrived, Boldt's guests were encouraged to explore the splendors of the new hotel, its private rooms and suites, its display of Venetian silk, Russian marble, and ornate furnishings that invoked the Medici, Versailles, and Napoleon's Empire. "Louis XIV," said a dazzled reporter from the *New York Sun,* "could not have got the like of the first suite of apartments set apart for the most distinguished guests of the hotel. Here is a canopied bed upon a dais, as a king's should be. Upon this couch shall repose the greatnesses and, looking about them, see many thousands of dollars' worth of fineries. Think of the joy of being great!" "So numerous were the conveniences," wrote Albert S. Crockett, a journalist whose beat was New York hotels, "so many and so appealing were the luxuries offered, and so widely were these read about and talked about, that in time, if a man wished to be of any importance when he came to New York, he simply had to stop at the Waldorf."

Opening-night charity patrons listened to a concert by Walter Damrosch's New-York Symphony Orchestra performing selections from Georges Bizet's *Carmen,* Richard Wagner's *Meistersinger,* and, somewhat less predictably, Max Bruch's *Kol Nidre.* Then the guests sat down to the supper Boldt's staff set out for them. It included oysters in béchamel sauce, cutlets of braised sweetbreads, terrapin, various pâtés, and other rich delicacies washed down with champagne and claret punch. Even a last-minute strike by workers in the pantry failed to disrupt the evening: an assistant steward mounted a behind-the-scenes rescue operation and recruited replacement dishwashers from men off the streets.

Boldt's opening event established a formula that has never lost its effectiveness: in a setting that invited glittering displays of gowns from Paris and jewels from Tiffany and Cartier, he brought together money, the upper class, fashion, good works, and upscale entertainment. A publicity and public-relations triumph, his opening night, "a brilliant social event," was the lead story on page one of the next day's *New York Times*. There, an article of five thousand words or so spilled over onto page two and listed the names of the more prominent guests, and described what some of them wore. It even included a tribute to the generosity of "Mr. Boldt, a gentleman who does not allow his wonderful energy to obscure his affability." He saw to it that the Waldorf, and soon after its larger twin, the Astoria, became both temples of pleasure and theaters of cultural and social life in a great city.

Jack had threatened at first to get back at his cousin by tearing down his mother's house and replacing it with a row of stables. It was both gratifying and reasonable for him to expect that a stable, in effect a hotel for horses, would turn away business from William's hotel next door. Jack's proposed stable, a millionaire's weapon in the real-estate and family wars, was clearly intended to be a thumb in William's eye, but solid money-shrewd sense prevailed. Jack canceled his stable plan, just as he had done with the stable he had planned to build next door to B'Nai Jeshurun and its anguished worshippers. He and his advisers realized that the

Waldorf, which was to gross over $4 million its first year, was a profitable venture.

Through troops of lawyers and accountants on both sides of the partition dividing the Astor estate office on Twenty-sixth Street, Jack negotiated an ad hoc alliance with William. Enlisting the Waldorf's architect, Henry Hardenbergh, and with Boldt as manager, he planned an abutting $3 million hotel to fill out the entire Fifth Avenue block front and considerable footage westward along Thirty-fourth Street. Harmonious in style with the Waldorf but much larger and several stories taller, Jack's hotel dwarfed, enveloped, and subsumed his cousin's, in outward appearance at least, a victory in their long-standing battle. He wanted to name it the Schermerhorn, after his mother's distinguished Old New York family. William, however, refused to allow even this vicarious honor to his aunt, the most powerful woman in American society. He persuaded Jack to settle instead on the name Astoria, after their ancestor's fur-trading post on the Columbia River. For the opening of the new hotel on November 1, 1897, Boldt staged another extravaganza that went on from noon to midnight, mixed charity, wealth, fashion, and entertainment, and generated columns of news coverage.

By the terms of a painfully hashed-out contract, corridors connecting the two buildings could be sealed off if the fragile truce, uncomfortable for both parties, failed to hold. The great double building was a house divided, like the Astor dynasty itself, which was riven by old resentments ripening into flagrant insults.*

---

*Only two years before these negotiations, William Waldorf had given a big dinner in London on the night [Jack's] sister, Mrs. James Roosevelt, lay dead in the city. Perhaps in retaliation the following year, when Mrs. William

But the house stood nonetheless and even flourished. The two buildings, married in name by a hyphen and known thereafter as the Waldorf-Astoria, opened for combined business in 1897 as the world's largest and most luxurious hotel. "Like New York itself," the historian Lloyd Morris wrote, "the Waldorf-Astoria crystallized the improbable and fabulous. It was more than a mere hotel. It was a vast, glittering, iridescent fantasy that had been conjured up to infect millions of plain Americans with a new idea—the aspiration to lead an expensive, gregarious life as publicly as possible." Combining forces and fortunes in their double hotel, the two otherwise warring Astor cousins created what Henry James was to describe as "a new thing under the sun" that gave him a glimpse of "perfect human felicity."

Waldorf's body was being returned to this country for burial, Ava and *the* Mrs. Astor appeared at the opera together. Society was shocked at the impropriety." Lucy Kavaler, *The Astors* (New York, 1966), 155.

FIVE

"A New Thing Under the Sun"

i.

IN THE LATE SUMMER OF 1904 Henry James came home from England for a ten-month visit. He had been gone for over twenty years, as long an absence as the sleep from which Rip Van Winkle, born a subject of King George III, awakened to find himself citizen of a new nation, the United States. Measured by the changes Henry James saw in the pace, feel, and institutions of daily life, a second American Revolution might as well have run its course since he had left.

Three recent novels—*The Wings of the Dove, The Ambassadors, The Golden Bowl*—certified him, at least in the view of a handful of critics and readers, as master in the house of fiction, just as he was, but without any doubt this time, master in his fastidiously regulated bachelor establishment, Lamb House, at Rye on the Sussex coast. A subtenant now occupied the property and enjoyed the sea air, garden study, flowering peach trees, and companionship of a ruby-colored dachshund, Maximilian, whose pedigree, James said, was as long as a typewriter ribbon. Maximilian's absent owner, meanwhile, was in transit, visiting a dozen and more American cities as he traveled from New England to Florida and from New York and Washington to California and the Pacific Northwest. He had gone on the lecture circuit, a routine occupation for many other literary celebrities and entertainers, but not something comfortable for this fierce exquisite who yearned for perfection but also needed to cover the expenses of his trip. Weaving seamless sentences that drifted like cigar smoke in the somnolent air of the lecture hall, he articulated the art of fiction to audiences in half a dozen American cities.

He extracted from his travels what he called "features of the human scene" and "properties of the social air." The self-styled "visionary tourist," "restless analyst," and "irrepressible story seeker" planned to study "the working of democratic institutions" as they "determine and qualify manners, feelings, communications, modes of contact, and conceptions of life." Three years later, with his gathered impressions plucked, cleaned, trussed, and done to a turn, he served them up, sauced with his celebrated qualifiers and discriminations, in a travel book *The American Scene*. If the title had not already been taken, he said, he could have called his book "The Return of the Native."

Like other visitors from abroad, James was overwhelmed by the rush and vehemence of turn-of-the-century American life, and, on one level, its immense wealth, extravagance, and ostentation. Nowhere was this display more flagrant than in New York, the nation's social, cultural, and financial capital. During the 1890s and a few years after, old John Jacob Astor's city of the future, where every square foot of land doubled in value year after year, had been the setting for social events that were Roman carnivals of gluttony, sottishness, and vulgar display: imitations of the royal courts of Europe, for example, and banquets that honored dogs, horses, and chimpanzees.

Mining, oil, steel, and railroad Golcondas had created a breed of sudden millionaires eager to enjoy and flaunt their wealth. They built French and Italian Renaissance palaces along Fifth Avenue and Madison Avenue and seasonal counterparts in the marble and granite "cottages" of Newport—tangible evidences, as James described them, of "witlessness" and "affronted proportion." For H. G. Wells, Newport's "triumphs of villa architecture in thatch and bathing bungalows in marble" sounded "the same note of magnificent irresponsibility" as the Manhattan residences of steel masters Andrew Carnegie and Henry Clay Frick, the Astors, Vanderbilts, Havemeyers, and Huntingtons. The owners of these palaces, Wells thought, were like children scattering toys on the playroom floor and leaving them there. A newly moneyed leisure class, although secure in its sense of self as commanding deference and privilege, nevertheless aspired to higher membership in a small, established nucleus, "society," founded on relatively "old" money.

Recognizing tectonic shifts in New York's social and physical landscape, Henry James felt dispossessed, uprooted, his past amputated, leaving him with a chill in his heart. His birthplace off Washington Square had vanished, torn down to make way for a nearby factory building that in March 1911 was to be the site of a fire in the Triangle Shirtwaist factory that took the lives of 146 workers, mostly Jewish immigrants. Trinity Church, long a commanding ornament of lower Broadway, cringed in the shadow of a steel-framed, elevator-served, twenty-story office building. Immigration and trade had transformed the town James remembered from his childhood as small, warm, and ingenuous, with some of the feel of a family party. His New York was now the largest Irish,

Italian, and Jewish city in the world. Surface and elevated lines and a new subway system that ran through 134 miles of tunnels webbed the city's sprawl.

The brick-and-limestone federal immigration center on Ellis Island served as the main portal through which a nation of 80 million admitted a million newcomers each year. The vast caravansary was a monument to the open-door policy, the nation's hunger for cheap labor, and its genius for assembly-line, rational organization on a heroic scale. Some days as many as 21,000 immigrants passed through Ellis Island's reception halls, refectories, dormitories with banks of steel beds, examination rooms, baths, chutes, and holding pens, its hospital, dental clinic, registries, currency exchange, and, at the end of the process, ticket office selling transportation to the sweatshops, mills, and wheat fields of the golden land. The overall impression, James wrote after touring Ellis Island as a guest of the commissioner, was that of a scientific feeding of the mill. "It is a drama that goes on, without pause, day by day and year by year, this visible act of ingurgitation on the part of our body politic and social, and constituting really an appeal to amazement beyond that of any sword-swallowing or fire-swallowing of the circus."

About five miles north of Ellis Island, on Fifth Avenue between Thirty-third and Thirty-fourth streets, stood a radically opposed but equally distinctive feature of American life. This was the Waldorf-Astoria, epitome of the fin de siècle luxury hotel and an expression of the American worship of bigness and rationality. This immense establishment comprised over a thousand guest rooms and half a hundred public rooms. Pleasure dome and social force, theater and theme park, the Astors' great hotel, the most expensive of its kind, was a place of artistic, mechanical, and

Wealth Incarnate:
The Founder, John Jacob
Astor (1763–1848), by
James Wesley Jarvis

(National Portrait Gallery,
Washington D.C.)

ABOVE: High Security: The Astor
Business Office, 85 Prince Street

LEFT: "Palais Royal": The
Founder's Astor House,
Broadway, opened 1836

(Brown Brothers)

Palmer House, Chicago, opened 1873. Rudyard Kipling said it was "a gilded and mirrored rabbit-warren." (Culver Pictures)

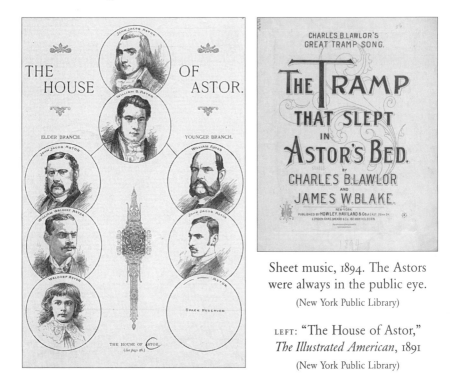

Sheet music, 1894. The Astors were always in the public eye.

(New York Public Library)

LEFT: "The House of Astor," *The Illustrated American*, 1891

(New York Public Library)

Queen of "the Four Hundred": Mrs. William Astor, the former
Caroline Webster Schermerhorn (The Metropolitan Museum of Art, Gift
of R. Thornton Wilson and Orme Wilson, 1949, [49.4])

840 Fifth Avenue, Residence of Caroline Astor and her son
John Jacob Astor IV (1864–1912). Present site of Temple Emanu-El
(Museum of the City of New York)

Caroline Astor's ballroom/gallery at 840 Fifth Avenue (Brown Brothers)

A celebrated beauty:
Ava Lowle Willing, the first
wife of John Jacob Astor IV

(Library of Congress)

Happy at last:
John Jacob Astor
IV and his second
wife, the former
Madeleine
Talmage Force

(Brown Brothers)

William Waldorf Astor and his wife, the former Mary Dahlgren Paul (New York Public Library)

RIGHT: New Netherland Hotel, Fifth Avenue and 59th Street, opened 1892 (Corbis)

LEFT: The Waldorf, opened 1893, towered over Caroline Astor's brownstone mansion on its right and forced her to move uptown. (Brown Brothers)

OPPOSITE: Waldorf-Astoria Hotel, Fifth Avenue and 34th Street, opened 1897, demolished in 1929 and replaced by the Empire State Building
(Museum of the City of New York)

ABOVE: Arrival at the
Waldorf-Astoria
(Brown Brothers)

LEFT: After dinner at the
Waldorf-Astoria
(Culver Pictures)

Expensive and
exclusive: The
Palm Garden
Restaurant,
Waldorf-Astoria
(Culver Pictures)

Annual Dinner of Cornell Alumni in New York and Vicinity, January 12, 1901

WALDORF-ASTORIA

BREAKFAST

Consommé en tasse

Mousse de Volaille, Vénitienne

Côtelettes d'Agneau, sautées, sauce Oporto
Haricots verts panachés

Bécassine Anglaise, rôtie
Salade Escarole

Glaces Assorties

Petits Fours

Café

The grand hotel was pleasure dome,
social center, and temple of gustation.

(New York Public Library)

Carte du Jour

Dinner of the Nassau Country Club
The Waldorf-Astoria
December 15th, 1906

WOMAN'S PRESS CLUB OF NEW YORK CITY
VALENTINE BREAKFAST MENU

Grape Fruit

Bouillon en Tasse
Olives   Celery   Radishes   Salted Almonds

Lobster à la Newburgh

Filet de Boeuf Mignonne Sauté
Pommes de Terre Croquette   Petit-Pois

Roast Squab on Toast
Salade Valentine

Fancy Ice Cream
Petit Fours

Café Noir

HOTEL ASTOR
FEBRUARY 17th 1906

Social theater: Lobby and Peacock Alley, Waldorf-Astoria (Museum of the City of New York)

RIGHT: Sheet music (New York Public Library)

The Bradley-Martin Ball at the Waldorf-Astoria, February 1897 (Museum of the City of New York)

Hotel Astor, Times Square, opened 1904 (Museum of the City of New York)

Advertisement: Cutaway rendering (Museum of the City of New York)

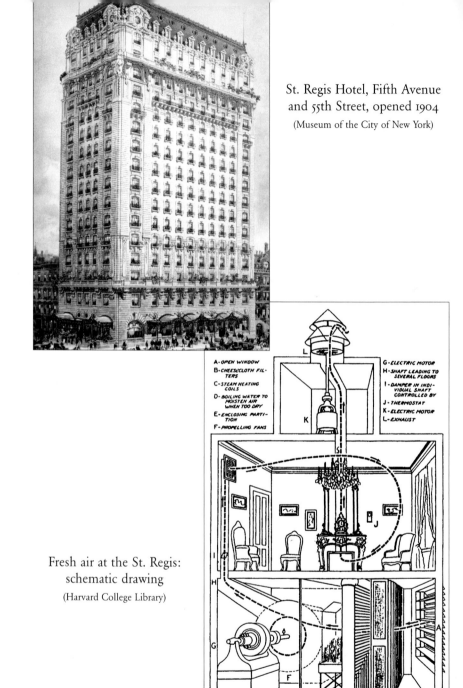

St. Regis Hotel, Fifth Avenue
and 55th Street, opened 1904

(Museum of the City of New York)

A - OPEN WINDOW
B - CHEESECLOTH FIL-
    TERS
C - STEAM HEATING
    COILS
D - BOILING WATER TO
    MOISTEN AIR
    WHEN TOO DRY
E - ENCLOSING PARTI-
    TION
F - PROPELLING FANS

G - ELECTRIC MOTOR
H - SHAFT LEADING TO
    SEVERAL FLOORS
I - DAMPER IN INDI-
    VIDUAL SHAFT
    CONTROLLED BY
J - THERMOSTAT
K - ELECTRIC MOTOR
L - EXHAUST

Fresh air at the St. Regis:
schematic drawing

(Harvard College Library)

Colonel John Jacob
Astor IV, about 1899
(Culver Pictures)

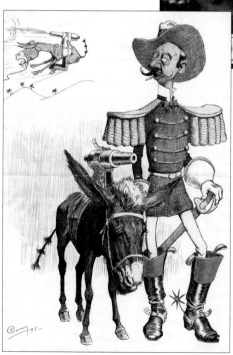

"A New Factor in Modern
Warfare: The Jack-Ass(tor)
Battery"
(New York Public Library)

John Jacob Astor IV at the boat train for the *Titanic* (Exclusive News Agency, London)

East Room, Waldorf-Astoria: Senate Committee meets to investigate
Titanic disaster (Library of Congress)

Seigneur of Cliveden and Hever Castle: the future viscount, William Waldorf Astor, by Sir Hubert von Herkomer
(Mary Evans/Image Works)

Tudor-style stronghold: William Waldorf Astor's office and pied-à-terre, 2 Temple Place, Victoria Embankment, London
(Justin Kaplan)

Cliveden, Upper Thames Valley, Berkshire (Justin Kaplan)

Cliveden's "Fountain of Love," by Thomas Waldo Story, commissioned by William Waldorf Astor (Justin Kaplan)

sybaritic wonders. Its splendor legitimized the open existence of an American leisure class. In its unashamed pride and opulence the Waldorf-Astoria declared that New York was now a world capital with a place in history like Athens, Rome, and London.

Loosely described as German (or "Dutch") Renaissance in style, the Waldorf-Astoria was topped with an eye-catching array of turrets, chimneys, and red-tiled gables, all producing an effect that was both quaint and homely. Internally even more than externally, the massive building showed that superfluity and sometimes gigantism (as exemplified by native strawberries and oysters) were themselves attractive goals. The ninety-five-foot-long ballroom, for example, was three stories high. Like Isaiah Rogers before him, the architect, Henry Janeway Hardenbergh, was the premier hotel builder of his era and would go on from the Waldorf-Astoria to build other landmark hotels like the exuberant Beaux-Arts Plaza (1907) in New York and the more restrained Copley Plaza (1910) in Boston. He had already set a pattern for residential luxury with his Dakota Apartments (1882), a brick-and-stone chateau crowned with a three-story mansard roof that dominated the West Side skyline. Visually and institutionally, his Dakota was a Manhattan icon even before the first tenants moved in, and this was true of both his Plaza Hotel and each of the two components of his Waldorf-Astoria.

Like the Dakota, the buildings Hardenbergh designed for the Astor cousins had a richly textured, multidimensional, picturesque cladding of balconies, arches, pilasters, bays, loggias, and alternating courses of terra-cotta, brick, and stone. His buildings had a touch of whimsy as well and disclosed nooks, turrets, and similar surprises that gave them the look of mammoth cuckoo clocks. In mood and style they were in the forefront of a general turning

away from the brownstone monotony and mournfulness of post–
Civil War New York, the "intolerable ugliness," as Edith Wharton
saw it, of a "low-studded rectangular" city "cursed with its universal chocolate-colored coating of the most hideous stone ever quar-
ried, this cramped horizontal gridiron of a town without towers,
porticoes, fountains, or perspectives." The Waldorf-Astoria was an
architectural lexicon of historical allusions and Beaux-Arts con-
ceits. Especially in its public rooms, Hardenbergh's hotel combined a caliph's palace with one of mad King Ludwig's Bavarian
castles.

Filling out the spaces assigned to them by the architect, hotel
decorators raided history and racked up enormous stylistic indebtedness to the Medicis and the Pharaohs, the Sun King's court and
Napoleon's Empire. Hotel decorators were theatrical set designers
at heart. Like D. W. Griffith and Cecil B. DeMille a little later on,
they provided the culturally untraveled with adventure, visual
thrills, a sense of history, and something of a museum and amusement park experience. Shortly after the end of World War II a flam-
boyant American architect named Morris Lapidus was to reconceive
the luxury hotel as a "movie set" in itself, a spectacle so over-
whelming that, he believed, people would "walk in and drop dead"
in astonishment at such sights as a lobby furnished with a full-scale
monkey jungle or a swamp of live alligators to remind guests, he
said, that "they were in Florida." He intended his Fontainebleau
and Eden Roc hotels in Miami Beach to fulfill "dreams of tropical
opulence and glittering luxury." His trademark features were weird
lighting, vibrant colors, birdcages on poles, floating ceilings punc-
tured by "cheese-holes," M. C. Escher–like flying stairways that
went nowhere, and a dizzying potion of French Provincial and
Italian Renaissance styles. As well as entertainment and surprise,

Lapidus's "palaces of kitsch" (as they were often called) provided a stage and backdrop for guests to show off gowns and jewels. Lapidus's boyhood visits to Coney Island's Luna Park had introduced him to fantasy architecture. Later, when he was an apprentice architect, a stay at the Palmer House in Chicago gave him a firsthand experience of the luxury hotel executed on a grand scale.

The Astors' double hotel built on the sites of their parents' mansions was indeed "a new thing under the sun," Henry James said. A writer of cool and appraising sentences as delicately equipoised as a jeweler's balance, the novelist, "a palpitating pilgrim," found himself in the grip of nothing short of a paroxysm of enthusiasm. The great hotel offered him, he wrote, "one of my few glimpses of perfect human felicity," and of "a social order in positively stable equilibrium." He had discovered "a world whose relation to its form and medium was practically imperturbable; here was a conception of publicity *as* the vital medium organized with the authority with which the American genius for organization, put on its mettle, alone could organize it. . . . a gorgeous golden blur, a paradise peopled with unmistakable American shapes." "There are endless things in 'Europe,' to your vision, behind and beyond the hotel, a multitudinous complicated life; in the States, on the other hand, you see the hotel as itself that life, as constituting for vast numbers of people the richest form of experience." Here at the Astors' great hotel was "a supreme social expression," "the essence of the loud New York story" of power, wealth, display, and spending. The "immense promiscuity" of the place—an unleashed social pluralism—broke down every barrier except "money and presentability" (which he tended to take for granted) and breached the wall between private and public life.

Avatar of modernity, the Astors' great and expensive hotel even had a leveling effect. Rich, famous, beautiful, and fashionable men and women, whose daily lives had in the past been led in private, were now to be seen enjoying the pleasures of ornate function rooms exposed to public view. Bathed in the full glare of attention, these rare creatures, the subject of news and gossip stories, were on display for ordinary citizens to observe and maybe learn from as part of their own education in polite customs and demeanor, all of this and more in preparation for a prospective climb up the ladder. At least from a distance, celebrities and society exotics could be seen dancing, entertaining one another at tea or at dinner in the glass-enclosed Palm Garden (in obligatory full evening dress), conversing in casual encounters in alcoves, mingling with fashionable young bucks and Wall Street titans in the men's café, or sipping Turkish coffee served them in the lobby by a genuine Turk and his boy assistant. "In such great hotels as the Waldorf-Astoria," H. G. Wells wrote, "one finds the new arrivals, the wives and daughters from the west and south, in new bright hats and splendors of costume. . . . From an observant tea-table beneath the fronds of a palm, I surveyed a fine array of these plump and pretty pupils of extravagance," acolytes of a religion of spending and flaunting. On ordinary days the Waldorf-Astoria's floating population was in the thousands, mostly composed of transient spectators in a three-hundred-foot-long, deep-carpeted, mirrored and amber marble corridor that invited and favored displays of finery and came to be known as Peacock Alley.

"Think of it!" said Robert Stewart, a journalist writing in 1899.

You arrive tired, dusty, irritable. Your bag is whisked out of your hand, and you are conducted through a brilliant hall . . .

Presto! You find yourself in a bijou of a suite, your trunks awaiting you, with a bed which simply beseeches you to lie on it, and with a porcelain tiled bathroom all your own. You press one button in the hall; electric lights flash up. You press another; a maid or valet . . . knocks to unpack your luggage and help you to dress. You press a third; a hall boy appears, like the slave of Aladdin's lamp, to execute any possible command monsieur may issue, from fetching a glass of iced water to ordering a banquet served up to you.

The great department stores of the late nineteenth century "democratized luxury," Emile Zola wrote, by offering ordinary people the opportunity to view and touch expensive goods of all sorts without obliging them to buy anything. In the same way, hotels such as the Waldorf-Astoria "brought exclusiveness to the masses" (said Oliver Herford, a contemporary wit) and allowed the masses to see how the other (the upper) half lived. The Waldorf-Astoria made dining and lunching in public fashionable, brought society out into the open, and inspired an age of lavish entertainments, parties, balls, and dinners—grand occasions previously confined to private houses.

The main restaurant's maître d', almost immediately famous as "Oscar of the Waldorf," was its Cerberus and absolute monarch. He introduced the velvet rope, a simple but remarkably effective device for flattering the elect and reminding outsiders of their outsiderness. The velvet rope created an instant atmosphere of privilege and a social economy of scarcity. Oscar also introduced the dining public to after-theater suppers, the chafing dish, lobster Newburg, chicken à la king, and trademark "Waldorf" salads of apples, nuts, celery, and mayonnaise. Even the chief house detective,

Captain Joe Smith, trained at Scotland Yard, was a celebrity and had a book written about his career as watchdog and gumshoe, *Crooks of the Waldorf.* "The Waldorf was his church," his biographer wrote, "and violation of its sanctity was a desecration."

The financiers, architects, and decorators of the great fin de siècle hotels had recognized in the American public a taste for luxury and social spectacle and turned this into a need. Far more than a convenience or commercial venture, the luxury hotel was a visionary attempt to create a world that was materially near-perfect down to its smallest details and workings, flattered the senses, anticipated and satisfied needs, and conferred status on anyone, guest or tourist, who entered its precincts. The private palaces of the robber barons of the Gilded Age had outgrown their limits and evolved into the grand hotel, an establishment bigger and grander and more impressive than any private palace: accessible and logical, organized from cellar scullery to roof garden on principles of comfort and display married to efficiency, ingenuity, fanatical attention to detail, technical improvement, and publicity. Combining the functions of marketplace and town square, the hotel lobby, only recently evolved from barroom and parlor, became one of the theaters of modern life.

In the early 1860s the British novelist Anthony Trollope noted that American hotels had a more central and expressive function in community life than in any other country he had visited and were built on a scale that seemed to him "unnecessarily extravagant." "In the States of America," he wrote, "the first sign of an incipient settlement is a hotel five stories high, with an office, a bar, a cloak-room, three gentlemen's parlors, two ladies' parlors, a ladies' entrance, and two hundred bedrooms. . . . When the new hotel rises up in the wilderness, it is presumed that people will come there with the express object of inhabiting it. The hotel itself will create a population." But the hotel cuisine of that time, he complained, featured grease, not gravy—"undisguised grease, floating in rivers, not grease caused by accidental bad cookery, but grease on purpose. . . . I never yet made a single comfortable meal at an American hotel."

Almost half a century later, Henry James argued that what he identified as "the hotel spirit may just *be* the American spirit most seeking and finding itself." Whatever deficiencies or betrayal of ideal he was to see in his rejected homeland, he discovered in the "amazing hotel world" a "synonym for civilization." He expected to write "brilliant chapters" on the subject of hotel life and considered himself qualified for the task not by gift alone but by a continuity of experience going back to his earliest years. This was when he and his siblings were "nothing less than hotel children" whisked by their restless father from one place to another. Among the many places James recalled from his childhood was a summer hotel on Staten Island, the Pavilion, that even toward the end of his life evoked images of "a great Greek temple shining over the blue waters in the splendor of a white colonnade and a great yellow pediment." Other hotels that remained lodged in his memory when he was seventy were the Hamilton House, on the south shore of Long Island; in New York, A. T. Stewart's Metropolitan, on lower Broadway; and the Clarendon on Broadway at Thirty-eighth Street, "then the latest thing in hotels" and favored by foreign visitors. But mostly he remembered the Astor House, the astonishing hotel on lower Broadway that old John Jacob Astor had built in 1836.

Usually critical and restrained in his responses to American life, James could hardly restrain his exclamations of wonder and discovery when he visited Henry Flagler's Breakers, Royal Poinciana, and Alhambra-like Ponce de Leon: these were "monster hotels," John Bunyan's Vanity Fair "compressed under one vast cover" and producing "the illusion of romance." In California he stayed at the Hotel del Monte in Monterey and, across the bay from San Diego, the Victorian gingerbread Hotel del Coronado, reputed to be the largest wooden structure in the world.

As far back as 1878, in his first popular success, *Daisy Miller,* James had claimed great hotels as a territory of the modern novelist. In a late (1910) story, "A Round of Visits," he described his fictional "Pocahontas"—a "great gaudy hotel"—as "a complete social scene in itself, on which types might figure and passions thicken and dramas develop, without reference to any other sphere, or perhaps even to anything at all outside."

The American hotel had become a forcing bed and popular setting for fiction. The original Astor House figures as landmark and measure of success in nearly every one of Horatio Alger Jr.'s immensely popular strive-and-succeed, pluck-and-luck stories. The heroine of Theodore Dreiser's *Sister Carrie,* a country girl from the Midwest, follows her rising star to success on the Broadway stage and a suite at the Waldorf-Astoria. Seated in her rocking chair by the window, she looks out on an "unending procession of carriages rolling up Fifth Avenue." Her former lover, meanwhile, has hit bottom and kills himself in a Bowery flophouse. Clyde Griffiths, in Dreiser's *An American Tragedy,* has his first, and fatally seductive, taste of luxury in the lobby of the Green-Davidson Hotel in Kansas City. "It was all so lavish. Under his feet was a checkered black and white marble floor. Above him a coppered and stained and gilded ceiling. And supporting this, a veritable forest of black marble columns."

Plucked from genteel poverty, Edith Wharton's Lily Bart (*The House of Mirth*) enters "the world of the fashionable New York hotel—a world over-heated, over-upholstered, and over-fitted with mechanical appliances for the gratification of fantastic requirements, while the comforts of a civilized life were as unattainable as in a desert." Wharton calls one of her generic establishments "The Emporium Hotel," another "The Stentorian." The windows of these places are triple-curtained, the rooms stifled in upholstery and "ornamental excrescence" bathed in a blaze of electric light. "Through this atmosphere of torrid splendor moved wan beings as richly upholstered as the furniture, beings without definite pursuits or permanent relations, who drifted on a languid tide of curiosity from restaurant to concert-hall, from palm-garden to music-room, from 'art exhibit' to dressmaker's opening."

Captive of extravagant fantasies, the victim-hero of Willa Cather's "Paul's Case" steals a thousand dollars from his employer in Pittsburgh and runs away to New York, where he takes a suite at the Waldorf and fulfills his visions of luxury: "the plot of all dreams, the text of all romances, the nerve-stuff of all sensations." "On every side of him towered the glaring affirmation of the omnipotence of wealth." He explores "the chambers of an enchanted palace, built and peopled for him alone." "Everything was quite perfect," and for the few days he spends at the Waldorf, Paul becomes "exactly the kind of boy he had always wanted to be," living "the sort of life he was meant to live." With his theft discovered and reported in the papers, he sees no way out of his delicious dream except to throw himself under the wheels of a train.

Vicki Baum's *Grand Hotel,* originally published in German as *Menschen im Hotel* (1929), was both an immensely popular novel and an all-star film (1932) with Greta Garbo, Joan Crawford, John Barrymore, and Lionel Barrymore. (A 1944 remake, *Weekend at the Waldorf,* starred Ginger Rogers and Lana Turner.) Baum had re-searched her story of romance, chicanery, broken hopes, and bed-room intrigue by working six weeks as a parlor maid in Berlin's fashionable Hotel Adlon. Her novel gave full play to the idea of the grand hotel as a social microcosm and literary archetype. Its cast of characters—faded ballerina, bankrupt baron, sluttish stenog-rapher—updated Sebastian Brant's fifteenth-century satire, *The Ship of Fools.* "Grand hotel. Always the same," her brandy-soaked Dr. Otternschlag says at the end. "People come, people go. Noth-ing ever happens." Novelists who adopted Baum's microcosm template with popular success included Arthur Hailey, whose *Hotel* (1965) dramatized the crises of daily life at the fictional St. Gregory in New Orleans. Hailey's novel enjoyed a later career as a movie and television series.

The hero of Steven Millhauser's Pulitzer Prize–winning novel, *Martin Dressler* (1996), is fascinated by the operational aesthetic of hotels, the way their complex systems work. He rises from bellboy to builder and presiding genius of a thirty-story dreamworld hotel, a place of wonders. His Grand Cosmo, dedicated to "Culture, Commerce, and Commodious Living," is an eighth wonder of the world. It "rendered the city unnecessary. For whether the Grand Cosmo was the city itself, or whether it was the place to which one longed to travel, it was a complete and self-sufficient world, in comparison with which the actual city was not merely inferior, but superfluous."

. . .

Life in a great social marketplace like the Waldorf-Astoria possessed an overheated quality, a vehemence and intensity that gave even trivial, vulgar, or meretricious appearances at least a passing aura of consequence. So long as he was presentable, in overstuffed lobbies and glittering corridors the hotel tourist was allowed to linger night afer night without having to spend a penny. The spectator was a vital part of the spectacle. There he could catch celebrities on the wing and maybe even rub feathers with them in passing. On some evenings he might even see the opulently arrayed Lillian Russell, weighing in at about two hundred pounds—"San Simeon in corsets," as A. J. Liebling described her—and her sometime paramour, financier and heavy feeder Diamond Jim Brady. Among other celebrities were Prince Henry of Prussia, the kaiser's brother, here on a semiofficial visit to christen a royal yacht on its launching from an American shipyard; and Horace Fletcher, the nutritional guru whose gospel of "Fletcherism" led thousands of Americans to believe they could fight obesity and dyspepsia by chewing each mouthful of solid food thirty-two times (once for each tooth) until it turned to liquid and, in his words, "swallowed itself." ("Fletcherism" is "the greatest thing that ever was," Henry James said in 1906. But a few years later he blamed it for his depression and "loathing" of food.)

In a specially furnished suite served by his own imported staff, the Japanese plenipotentiary Baron Jutaro Komura hammered out terms of the Treaty of Portsmouth (1905) that ended the war with Russia (his opposite number in the negotiations, Minister Sergius Witte, stayed a mile uptown at the new St. Regis). The French engineer and international intriguer, Philippe Bunau-Varilla, called his customary room on the eleventh floor "the cradle of the Panama Republic." There he plotted the insurrection and drafted the treaty that eventually gave the United States control of the Panama Canal. Populist political leader and celebrated orator William Jennings Bryan often ate in the hotel café. Following the habits of his early years in the Midwest, he declined the fancy French-style offerings that were the pride of the house and ordered instead large farm-style meals of fried beefsteaks (or sometimes ham and eggs), German fried potatoes, and a loaf of bread, all of this washed down with two jugs of water.

One night financier and stock market plunger John W. "Betcha-a-million" Gates, a former dealer in hardware and barbed wire, sat down to a frugal supper of milk and crackers in the café and announced to his waiter that he had just made another million on the Street. Gates's sobriquet supposedly derived from a gambling game he invented one rainy afternoon: as if they were ponies, he started betting on raindrops moving down the windowpane. He habitually bet large sums of money on any proposition on which he thought he had a better-than-even chance. Gates's gambling headquarters were located in his regular suite at the hotel. Among those who sat in on his poker games were coke and steel magnate Henry Clay Frick, who had yet to build his private art palace on Fifth Avenue, and Gates's business partner, Colonel John Lambert, former warden of the Joliet, Illinois, penitentiary. One of Gates's poker games, begun in his private railroad car on the way from Chicago and continued on arrival in New York, went on virtually day and night for a week, with meals brought directly to the poker table. At the end about $500,000 changed hands, $300,000 of it coming from the pockets of Joseph Leiter, the Chicago wheat speculator.

In Gates's suite Frick, J. P. Morgan, Andrew Carnegie, and Elbert Gary first floated the idea of forming United States Steel, the world's first billion-dollar corporation. The "Waldorf Crowd," as it came to be known, consisted of wealthy speculators, most of them westerners, willing to follow Gates's lead. They had their own wire-service operators there and employed a network of agents to supply them with insider information and early election returns. There was a constant buzz of money talk: the Waldorf-Astoria's barroom and men's café had become an extension of the trading floor of the New York Stock Exchange.

In September 1899 the nation welcomed back to its shores the conquering hero of the Spanish-American War, Admiral of the Navy George Dewey. From his flagship, the cruiser *Olympia,* in Manila Bay, he had issued an order that became almost instantaneously famous: "You may fire when you are ready, Gridley." In the annals of naval warfare his order took its place with David Farragut's "Damn the torpedoes!" and Horatio Nelson's "England expects every man will do his duty." Without losing a ship or a man (except for an engineer who died of heat prostration), Dewey's squadron destroyed the naval forces of Spain, captured Manila, and avenged the sinking of the *Maine.* Although the battle, interrupted by a pause for breakfast, had been more like a turkey shoot than "the Greatest Naval Engagement of Modern Times," Dewey's entry into New York City on the twenty-eighth was like the triumphs ancient Rome granted victorious emperors and generals. Dewey's *Olympia* led a two-and-a-half-mile-long parade of ships up the Hudson River and anchored opposite Grant's Tomb. That night, fireworks in the sky traced a thousand-square-foot portrait of the hero. The Waldorf-Astoria, the city's premier social venue, staged a monster reception—it started in the evening and continued through the next morning—for the most celebrated person who had ever passed through its doors.

Months earlier there had been fevered talk of Dewey as a presidential candidate in 1900, and he might well have been nominated, if he had not been addicted to blurting. He had barely survived a public-relations disaster when he said to a man he scarcely knew, "Our next war will be with Germany." He hadn't realized, he said later, that the person he made this prediction to was a newspaper reporter who knew a story when he heard one. Dewey did not survive the next disaster. Finally announcing his availability as a presidential candidate, he explained that after long and careful study he had concluded that "the office of President is not such a very difficult one to fill, his duties being mainly to execute the laws of Congress. Should I be chosen for this exalted position I would execute the laws of the Congress as faithfully as I have always executed the orders of my superiors." "I don't understand how I got the idea in the first place," he said later. Afloat on billows of public laughter, the admiral sailed into America's Valhalla of forgotten heroes.

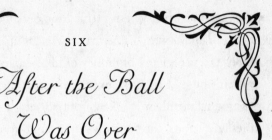

SIX

After the Ball Was Over

i.

DURING THE WINTER OF 1896–1897 the United States was mired in a period of economic distress and widespread unemployment that had begun with a Wall Street panic in 1893. Financiers, businessmen, and members of the clergy denounced a growing socialist, trade union, and protest movement as a threat to order, decency, and what remained of national prosperity. At a cost of much violence and bloodshed, President Grover Cleveland sent federal troops to Chicago to put down a strike at the Pullman Sleeping Car Company that had halted rail traffic in the Midwest and elsewhere. Meanwhile homeless men lined up at soup kitchens in the streets of New York and Chicago. In January 1897 a socially prominent couple, Mr. and Mrs. Bradley Martin, sent out about a thousand invitations to a private costume ball at the Waldorf. The party was to cost its sponsors and guests an estimated total of $500,000, roughly equivalent to $7 million in current purchasing power.

Mrs. Martin, the former Cornelia Sherman, was the only child of Isaac Sherman and his wife. Enjoying comfortable retirement from the leather and fancy wood business, Sherman was generally thought to be worth a respectable $200,000. Cornelia and her husband, Bradley, who came from a rich upstate manufacturing family and had plenty of money of his own, lived with her parents in their house at 20 West Twentieth Street. Relatively inconspicuous young members of New York society, homebound in their tastes and habits, the young Martins raised four children and were not known for giving parties or fancy entertainments.

When Isaac Sherman died in 1881 probate revealed to everyone's surprise that he had been a very rich man. To his widow he left a comfortable annuity, but to Cornelia he left about $7 million, an amount not in the Astor and Vanderbilt league but sufficient, especially when supplemented by Cornelia's husband's fortune, to allow her to have nearly everything she wanted. In time this included ownership of Marie Antoinette's crown jewels, occupancy of a hunting, shooting, and fishing estate at Balmacaan on Loch Ness, and a reputation for giving spectacular parties. Sudden wealth had the effect on Cornelia of a burr under her saddlecloth. Soon after Isaac's funeral at All Souls' Unitarian Church and an obligatory month of mourning she whipped herself up from a demure walk around the New York social track to a full gallop.

She and Bradley bought the house next door to her parents', took a long European trip, and during their absence abroad had the walls between the houses knocked down and the two converted into a mansion suitable for grand entertainments. They staffed it with an English butler, several liveried footmen, and a corps of other household servants. Cornelia's regular presence at fashionable events began to be noted in the press. Gorgeously got up as Mary Stuart (and wearing Mary Stuart's diamond tiara), despite her dumpiness, Cornelia was one of the more admired guests at Alva Vanderbilt's fancy-dress ball in the winter of 1883. This was the showiest and most expensive event of its kind (estimates ran to a quarter of a million dollars) that New York had ever seen, "a walking jewelry store," as one reporter was to describe a comparable event. LIKE AN ORIENTAL DREAM, the *New York Herald* headlined its story, THE WEALTH AND GRACE OF NEW YORK IN VARIED AND BEAUTIFUL ARRAY. Soon after this triumph, members of Cornelia's circle and the gossip columns of the city's newspapers began to hear about a new purpose she had found for her life. One day, she said, she herself would give a costume ball surpassing Alva Vanderbilt's in dazzle and expense and thereby clinch a high place in New York's social royalty. In one of several lavish rehearsals for her costume ball, in 1885 she roofed over the gardens of the Twentieth Street mansion and staged an evening entertainment that confirmed her place in the front rank of contenders for the crown.

During the decade-and-a-half run-up to her climactic bid for the summit Cornelia generated yards of newspaper copy. She organized a Christmas Eve surprise party to pay tribute to Caroline Astor, undisputed leader of New York society. About a hundred celebrants drove uptown in their carriages from Cornelia's mansion to *the* Mrs. Astor's ballroom, which had been elaborately garnished, somehow unnoticed by her (or so it was claimed), with immense masses of holly, white carnations, and white violets. Even the normally aloof William Waldorf Astor, wearing a white fur-trimmed Santa Claus cap, put aside his chronic enmity to Caroline and joined her delegation this evening. A few months later he also attended Cornelia's dinner party and cotillion for nearly three hundred blue bloods at Delmonico's. The men that evening went home with party favors, chosen by Cornelia, of jeweled daggers and replicas of the ancient Order of the Golden Fleece. Her entertainments, said the *New York Times*, "have become famous in society for their lavishness of expense and richness of appointment."

It was at about this time, on the eve of their annual sailing to London for the social and sporting season there, that Cornelia and her husband, the couple formerly known as Mr. and Mrs. Bradley Martin, sprouted a hyphen in their surname, somewhat like a supernumerary nipple, and, in parallel fashion to the orthographic coupling of the Waldorf and the Astoria hotels, began to call themselves the Bradley-Martins. In a similar status uptick they followed the virtually hallowed practice of their class by acquiring for their daughter an impecunious but titled mate, the twenty-five-year-old fourth Earl of Craven. A secure room in the basement of the Bradley-Martin mansion, which had been several times a fat target for burglars, now held, it was announced to the press, some $200,000 worth of gold and silver wedding gifts.

In one season at their well-stocked estate on Loch Ness the sporting members of the family and their guests dispatched about six thousand head of game, including fifty-five stags. During their annual stays abroad, the Bradley-Martins were said to have "equaled all previous records set by rich Americans in the entertaining line." When the family returned to New York in December 1894 on the White Star *Teutonic*, they were accompanied by one servant for each member, another servant for each of the half dozen and more steamer trunks, and an additional forty pieces of luggage. Back in their mansion on Twentieth Street, Cornelia and her husband, by this time veterans of publicity and aware of its enhanced value when withheld, declined to talk to representatives of the press and had the butler turn them away at the front door. "I don't see what there is to interview them about," her brother-in-law, Frederick Townsend Martin, explained to a reporter who walked with him up Fifth Avenue on the way to the Union Club. "They have simply come back as any other travelers from Europe might do, and are to take up their old life here in just about the same way as they left it."

"Only more so," he could have added: his sister-in-law Cornelia was soon to make her grand move and issue invitations to a fancy costume ball to take place on February 10, 1897. On her orders, the entire two lower floors of the Waldorf, crammed with flowers, mirrors, and tapestries, were to be transformed—inevitably, given the taste of the period—into the Versailles of Louis XIV and Louis XV. She asked her guests to costume themselves as aristocrats, nobles, and famous figures of the sixteenth, seventeenth, and eighteenth centuries. This excursion into gilded history provoked a competitive display of diamonds and heirloom pieces, some of which were bought or borrowed for the occasion; others, retrieved from bank vaults, had not been seen in public since the Vanderbilt ball. Cornelia regarded the announcement of her ball to be a much-needed stimulant to trade in a depression year. It immediately drove up the price of goods and services supplied by costumers, seamstresses, caterers, jewelers, wig makers, hairdressers, milliners, shoemakers, tailors, dancing masters, florists, antiquarians, fencing masters, and even armorers. Several guests planned to wear swords, and one, Oliver Hazard Perry Belmont, Alva Vanderbilt's new husband, reportedly paid $8,000 (in 1897 dollars) for a museum-quality breastplate of steel inlaid with gold, under which he planned to wear a Henry VIII velvet costume with ruffled sleeves.

"Future generations," said the gossip sheet *Town Topics*, "will date every event in relation to the Bradley-Martin ball." Soon after the invitations went out Cornelia's private affair became a public event discussed not only in the clubs and restaurants of New York and London but in factories, shops, business offices, pulpits, and probably mine shafts as well. But beneath the buzz of gossip rumbles of discontent and protest began to be heard.

William Stephen Rainsford, rector of St. George's, a fashionable Protestant Episcopal church on Stuyvesant Square at Sixteenth Street and Second Avenue, had a well-founded although tactfully moderated liberal reputation. He gave his blessing to the labor movement, social reform, the institutional accountability of the church, dancing in the parish house, toleration of saloons as refuge and comfort of the working class, and other progressive causes. His programs enjoyed the moral and financial support of Pierpont Morgan, the church's senior vestryman. A charismatic preacher who adored the spotlight, in late January Rainsford made one of his frequent bids for public attention. He gave an extended interview to a reporter from the *New York Times;* his subject, the Bradley-Martin ball. He declined to say whether he had advised his parishioners not to attend, but he conceded that such ostentatious display in a difficult time was "ill-advised," at least for practical reasons. It was bound to furnish ammunition to "socialistic agitators," "demagogues," "sentimentalists," and other such mischief makers busily and irresponsibly stirring up discontent with the existing social and economic order. Rainsford had in mind, to name two of the most prominent of these mischief makers, Pullman strike leader Eugene V. Debs, a recent convert to socialism, and William Jennings Bryan, a declared enemy of Wall Street. Although decisively defeated in the electoral vote in his campaign for the presidency against Republican William McKinley, Bryan, running on a platform of radical agrarianism and opposition to big business, had polled an ominous (in Rainsford's view) six million popular votes.

When asked whether he'd prefer to see great accumulations of wealth either hidden from public view or given to charity, Rainsford said such questions were beside the point. He concerned himself not with the morality of wealth but with its public relations. "New York is now credited by outsiders with being ostentatious, luxurious, and unpatriotic," he explained, carefully avoiding any reference to Christian precepts against laying up treasures on earth. "I think such charges are untrue, and I think the bringing of them is injurious to the entire country and to New York. . . . What I may have advised any members of my congregation . . . is nobody's business but mine and theirs—certainly not a matter for public discussion."

In both the United States and England, however, Rainsford's ethical gymnastics made him a source of amusement: here was a clerical dude who played to the grandstand and ended up making the ball an event of much greater consequence than it might have been if he had kept his mouth closed. But at least he stirred up earnest discussion about whatever obligations the rich had to the poor and to their own salvation. Not quite ten years earlier Andrew Carnegie had told readers of the *North American Review* that it was a disgrace for a rich man to die rich instead of giving his money away to libraries, foundations, and other good causes. On the other hand, was it possible that extravagant spending and ostentatious display could actually be good deeds? They stimulated the economy, created jobs, and trickled money down to the pockets of the working poor. At least this was the reasoning that shielded the Bradley-Martins from any pangs of conscience.

ii.

FEARING PROTEST demonstrations and possible violent acts by anarchists, the Waldorf management ordered workmen to board up the windows on the lower two stories. The night of February 10 perhaps two hundred police, some in plain clothes, surrounded the building, lined the sidewalks from Fifth Avenue to Broadway, and barricaded the street in front of the hotel, all these measures taken over public protests against unwarranted protection of the rich and blocking of free access to the streets. Theodore Roosevelt, then president of the board of police commissioners, said all such complaints of unfairness and inconvenience were "nonsense" and claimed he would have ordered the same sensible measures if the occasion had been instead "a clambake or picnic on the east side." Ten of his tallest men flanked the narrow passage from the curb to the draped doorway of the Waldorf on Thirty-third Street. The Bradley-Martins, who were reported to have received death threats, arrived at their party accompanied by two bodyguards. The United States Marine Band, brought in from Washington, sounded a fanfare and played through the long evening, occasionally relieved by Victor Herbert's band and a Hungarian Gypsy ensemble.

Gowned as Mary Queen of Scots, festooned with Marie Antoinette's crown jewels, including a massive ruby necklace, and seated on a throne as she received her guests, Cornelia could have been a model for Sir John Tenniel's picture of the Duchess in *Alice in Wonderland*. Her husband, dressed as Louis XV, stood at her side. He wore a suit of pink and white brocaded satin, knee breeches, white silk hose, low red-heeled shoes with diamond buckles, and a powdered wig. Jack Astor, appointed king of the ball by Cornelia, came in a relatively modest courtier's costume, but he carried a sword with a jeweled hilt and had a jeweled chain around his neck. (His absent cousin, William Waldorf Astor, was long since settled in England with his family.) Jack's wife, Ava, came as Marie Antoinette. In a velvet dress copied from a Van Dyck portrait, Caroline Astor, Jack's mother, wore a carapace of diamonds that flowed down her front from scalp to stomach.

By rough count, among the other costumed guests were ten Mmes. De Pompadour, eight Mmes. De Maintenon, three Catherines the Great, several other Marie Antoinettes, and dozens of Watteau women and Dresden figurines. Almost one hundred men came as Louis XV, and there were a Richelieu or two, a Dutch burgomaster à la Rembrandt, several toreadors, a sprinkling of sheikhs and mandarins, and a number of others in three-cornered hats, apparently the leavings of the city's costume shops. Pierpont Morgan's spirited daughter Anne came as Pocahontas, in a feathered dress made for her by American Indians. A young Mr. Cushing of Boston, rumored to be an artist, came as an Italian falconer of the fifteenth century: under a short jacket he wore white tights that left little to the imagination and drew stares and polite giggles. The revelers did not include impersonators of Charlotte Corday, the unfortunate Louis XVI, or any such grim reminders that many of these historical figures, and perhaps their impersonators as well, danced on a volcano.

As the long evening of dining, drinking, dancing, and posing for formal portraits stumbled toward four in the morning, several courtiers tripped over their swords and as a last resort tucked them under their arms. Stanford White was seen in lecherous and drunken pursuit of a young beauty named Mrs. Starr. In addition to generous quantities of whiskey, brandy, and still wines, Cornelia Bradley-Martin's guests consumed sixty cases of a Moët & Chandon champagne that a local historian recalled as "the most expensive sparkling wine known in the United States in 1897."

After the ball was over, it would have been reasonable to ask if anyone had a good time, and there were relatively few after-the-event reports on that point. But the evening left a general impression, according to the papers, that the great ball did not live up to its billing either in the degree of general happiness that prevailed, the number of guests (only about seven hundred) who actually attended, or how it stacked up against the Vanderbilt event. Nor was there either then or later any agreement on how much the whole thing had cost hosts and guests as a group. Cornelia's direct bill from the hotel for drink, food, and music came to a bargain $10,000, but this probably reflected a concession from the management and did not include trees and shrubs, Versailles panels and backdrops, banks of hothouse flowers, and pyramids of hothouse fruit. More significant, it did not even begin to reflect the sums Cornelia and her guests laid out for gowns, costumes, wigs, hairdos, jewels, accouterments, liveries for footmen and waiters, and the like.

"Half a million dollars gone up in frippery and flowers," wrote the fire-breathing iconoclast William Cowper Brann, but the "bedizened gang" at the Waldorf did not, he claimed, have half the fun a cow yard of hayseeds would have had at a taffy pull or corn husking. "Mrs. Bradley-Martin has triumphed gloriously," Brann went on, "raised herself by her own garters to the vulgar throne of Vanity." The evening's aftermath was a long collective hangover, a mood of glumness, ennui, and dull resentment only briefly relieved by a burlesque of the "Bradley Radley Ball" staged by the showman Oscar Hammerstein.

The great event had proved to be so blatant and heartless in its abdication of taste and social conscience that public opinion, along with a punitive doubling of their tax assessment, eventually pushed the Bradley-Martins into exile or, as they thought of it, preferred residence in England. Two years after the ball they emptied their house on Twentieth Street and shipped the furnishings to London. In the last of their several farewells to New York society they gave a banquet for eighty-six of their friends at the Waldorf-Astoria. The guests consumed green turtle soup, timbales of shad roe, and mignons of spring lamb while the hotel orchestra played Spanish melodies and popular black songs, among them a particular favorite of those in attendance, "If You Ain't Got No Money, You Needn't Come 'Round."

Wearing a gold-trimmed brocade-and-velvet suit and a powdered wig, Bradley-Martin's brother, Frederick Townsend Martin, had been a favored and apparently compliant guest at the ball. Clubman, cosmopolite, connoisseur, and confirmed bachelor, he had attended and kept track of many comparable events and knew what he was talking about when he rated them. In 1911 he published his observations in an alarmingly titled book, *The Passing of the Idle Rich*. It went over with the public and was so visual in its anecdotes that it lent itself to vaudeville burlesques and satiric dramatizations on the stage. In the intervening years he had become—or at least, as a published author, found it profitable to appear to be—a reproachful observer of the social scene, a combination of the Prophet Jeremiah and Banquo's ghost. It was clear from the thrust and texture of his argument that he had also read and absorbed *The Theory of the Leisure Class,* Thorstein Veblen's profoundly subversive analysis of the manners of the upper-class "barbarians" (as Veblen called them) who led American society.

One sentence of Veblen's about the leisure class could have served as a motto for Frederick Martin's book and an epitaph for his sister-in-law's carnival: "Conspicuous consumption of valuable goods is a means of reputability." *The Passing of the Idle Rich* served up vivid instances and dire predictions about the fate of a social class which, Martin said, had "sunk to the level of the parasite" and was "condemned to death."* He included the fashionable practice of dining out at great hotels among the many dreary schemes "devised to keep us from being bored to death by the mere fact of living." Among his dozen or so instances of colorful and indicative behavior on the part of the idle rich were Chicago gas company heir C. K. G. Billings's dinner served on horseback on the fourth floor of Sherry's Restaurant with waiters dressed as grooms; a birthday dinner for a black-and-tan dog, among whose presents was a diamond collar worth $15,000; Mrs. Stuyvesant Fish's dinner honoring a monkey in a full dress suit; a millionaire who had his dentist drill two rows of diamonds into his teeth; several "Jack Horner" dinners, one hosted by Stanford White, another served in tribute to Diamond Jim Brady: greeted by drunken

---

*By 1913, when he published a second book, a memoir titled *Things I Remember,* Martin had changed his tune. "I cannot conceive why this entertainment should have been condemned.... I was highly indignant about my sister-in-law being so cruelly attacked, seeing that her object in giving the ball was to stimulate trade, and, indeed, she was perfectly right.... Many New York shops sold out brocades and silks which had been lying in their stock-rooms for years." Man-about-town Martin sometimes supplemented his income with fees from the management for steering customers to the Plaza Hotel.

applause a small flock of canaries and nightingales emerged from a giant pie, followed by a naked girl.

But it was the example of his own brother and sister-in-law that Frederick saved for the concluding flourish in his register of the outré and the unpardonable: "One of the most lavish and expensive—probably the most expensive—dinners ever given in America was a hyphenated feast, the record of which is writ large upon the annals of metropolitan society." The great hotel built by the two warring Astor cousins had provided both opportunity and impetus for such presumably terminal antics of "the idle rich."

SEVEN

Aladdin

i.

Bʏ 1891, ᴡʜᴇɴ he turned forty-three and moved to England for good, William Waldorf Astor had cut himself free from all but his business ties to New York and his rejected homeland. His parents were dead, and his inheritance, loosely estimated to be between $150 million and $300 million, made him, like the founding Astor, one of the richest men alive. His wife, Mamie, to whom he had been genuinely devoted, died of peritonitis in 1894, at thirty-six. When he brought her body from London back to New York for burial in the Astor vault at Trinity Cemetery, he severed a last close tie to his earlier life. The House of Astor remained so split that neither his cousin Jack nor his aunt Caroline attended the burial services.

William could now live exactly as he wished. He kept an affectionate, indulgent, but generally distant eye on his children. The daily burden of seeing after their needs and schooling fell on a staff of nannies and tutors. A widower with unlimited means, he was in vigorous good health, except for attacks of gout, the rich man's disease thought to be brought on by rich food and flowing wines, both of which he not only enjoyed in a discriminating way but carefully ordered in daily instructions to his household staff.

Fair-haired with piercing blue eyes, he was handsome, in a formal, somewhat forbidding way, attractive to women and taking pleasure in their company.

For all his advantages, this Astor scion was one of the more unmerry creatures cast up out of the boil of heredity, nurture, endowment, and accident. Often the joke was on him: his career in politics a failure, his cobbled genealogy and literary efforts ridiculed along with his anomalous position as a "former American." Soon his missteps in British society, along with an undisguised and increasing eagerness to enter the peerage, were to make him a further butt for ridicule. The entry in the current *Oxford Dictionary of National Biography* writes him off as "shy, austere, and, by all accounts, unlovable. . . . He despised his native country and said so in print. In return, he was lampooned by the New York press." He had never been altogether able to shed the theology of unworthiness and damnation that his parents and nursemaids had drilled into him from childhood. But along with this joyless creed, and sometimes violently at odds with it, he had also inherited an unshakable sense of being in the first rank of the blue-blood elect. His wealth reinforced this, and so did his clear superiority to most of his social peers in intellect and cultivation. He had a passion for splendor and for building, and by his hotels left his mark on New York's architectural and social style.

He especially looked down on his younger cousin Jack, whom he regarded as a dilettante and playboy absorbed in the mindless pleasures of the very rich—clubs, yachts, racehorses, summers at Newport. Jack seemed to enjoy playing puppy dog to his powerful mother and his self-indulgent wife, the first of whom doted on him, while the other openly despised him. William's imagination lived in a landscape of palaces, castles, great estates, domains of

Tudors and the Medici; Jack's, in his inventor's workshop at Fern-cliff, his collection of motorcars, and a future shaped by science and religion. In their social and domestic traffic with the present, both Astors suffered from inexpressiveness. William in particular had a capacity for silence and isolation along with a thickening crust of reserve and a habit of making brusque and ill-considered responses to what he saw as challenges to his dignity. But with a few men and women whom he respected he could be gentle and open. At least on his own narrowly restrictive terms he had a certain gift for intimacy. "My father was not at all hard hearted, in fact he was very sensitive," his daughter Pauline said. "I often felt he needed help and sympathy, and yet it seemed impossible to reach him through his defenses of reserve and a certain aloofness. . . . His true self seldom appeared and his motives were often misjudged."

On an Atlantic crossing aboard the White Star liner *Majestic* he met Amy Small Richardson, an American woman married to a Washington, D.C., doctor. Over a period of five years, as a friend of both members of the couple and with no suggestion of attempted romance with the wife, he sent her dozens of candid and relaxed letters telling about his travels, his plans for perfecting his estates, family affairs. "I have seen my new granddaughter several times," he wrote in 1907, "and I am told she looks like me and has my ingratiating smile." The two shared an educated passion for gardens, architecture, and Tudor history. He sent her his stories, including one about his long past but never to be forgotten Italian "love adventure." "It will amuse you," he told her, "to see what your fellow traveler on the *Majestic* was like in those remote days." One Christmas he had Tiffany and Company in New York send her a tiny chain purse: "As it comes from Aladdin, it can never be empty," he wrote. Aladdin also sent her gifts of books and pictures, sprays of calla lilies and violets, and at least once a sum of money for her garden in Washington. "Do not thank me for the cheque, please, it makes me feel foolish to be thanked." At least momentarily, in such private encounters he could feel his virtually matchless wealth to be an irony of circumstance, even an embarrassment.

"I don't like your English aristocracy," he confided to his friend Lady Dorothy Nevill, the doyenne of London hostesses. "They are not educated, they are not serious." Nevertheless, English aristocracy and English titles affected him like strong drink. He collected dukes, duchesses, and other titled folk—in his view the only fit company for an Astor—the way he collected art and antiquities. He had little difficulty working his way into the circle of the pleasure-loving Prince of Wales, the future Edward VII. The prince was notorious for his reliance on his smart-set coterie of bankers and South African mining millionaires to get him out of debt. "I have never been directly asked to assist him financially," Astor told Amy Richardson, "nor have I done so." But at the very least the prince had held him in reserve. In 1896 "Wealthy Willie," as Astor was sometimes referred to in print, was reported to be engaged to marry Lady Randolph Churchill, the recently widowed mother of twenty-two-year-old Winston Churchill. "Mr. Astor's attentions to Lady Randolph Churchill have been so marked as to create no small amount of gossip," Harold Frederic reported to the *New York Times* from London. Lady Churchill, the former Miss Jennie Jerome of Brooklyn, had many admirers, including the Shah of Persia (who cooled on the affair after deciding she wasn't fat enough for his taste). She was dazzled by Astor's money and social status, but nothing came of this, nor of a second rumor linking him with the Countess of Westmoreland, who proved to be companionably married to the earl. Of more consequence was to be William's fevered, quasi-operatic romance, in 1913, when he was sixty-five, with the beautiful and sexually liberated Lady Victoria Sackville.

As a London residence for his children and himself, Astor bought 18 Carlton House Terrace, overlooking St. James's Park. It was already celebrated as one of the most elegant private houses in London, but, in his accustomed style, he had it thoroughly refurbished, added paneling, frescoes, and tapestries, and ordered a forty-foot-long table made for the enormous dining room. He offered what was reported to be a "fabulous" sum of money to rent, for just two days, a London house on the line of the parade and procession celebrating Queen Victoria's sixty years on the throne in June 1897. His offer astounded the noble owner, who accepted without hesitation. "Mr. Astor, in his entertaining, his residences, and his stables, is handsomely living up to the foreign reputation of Americans for extravagance," a *New York Times* editorial commented. "Perhaps, also, he is vainly endeavoring to live up to his income."

For his London business headquarters, and private retreat where he entertained casual women friends, he bought the building on Victoria Embankment at 2 Temple Place. He spent about $1.5 million converting it into a crenellated Tudor-style stronghold that assured him the maximum of isolation while serving as a private museum for his notable collection of paintings, autographs, books (including Shakespeare folios), and antique musical instruments. The interiors of Temple Place were more opulent than those of his London residence. The study in the main hall was over seventy feet long; two ornate chandeliers hung from its thirty-five-foot-high roof of hammer-beamed Spanish mahogany; Persian rugs and tiger skins softened the relative austerity of the inlaid marble floors.

"There is no more curious room in London," a local architect wrote, "than this hall which was intended by its creator to be a sort of temple of culture and expresses in a curious way his own tastes in art and literature." William hung a portrait of himself by Hubert von Herkomer on the wall along with portraits of the founding Astor and successors. Not an inch of door surfaces, walls, ceilings, and stairwells was left bare of carving, paneling, or other decorations. Wooden figures of the Four Musketeers stood guard on the newel posts. His writing table, carefully preserved by him over the years, was exactly as he had used it, ornaments and all, at the legation in Rome. An Italian fortune-teller had told him back then that his life was in danger. Her warning, along with the vulnerability inherent in the possession of wealth, had made him fearful of kidnappers and assassins with designs on him and his children. He kept a loaded pistol on the bedside table in his pied-à-terre and equipped the building with a security system that allowed him, by pressing a button, to lock and bar all windows and entrances (at the same time effectively, he must have recognized, keeping an intruder from escaping).

An antique New England spinning wheel stood near his desk in the office library. The main hall displayed a frieze depicting characters from *The Scarlet Letter, The Last of the Mohicans,* and "Rip Van Winkle," "all old friends of mine," he called them. He was also a devoted reader of *Leaves of Grass.* The weather vane was a brilliantly gilded replica of one of Columbus's caravels. It symbolized the linking, by discovery and commerce, of the Old World from which John Jacob Astor had come and the New World where he made his fortune. As fervently as he tried to make the opposite true, to the British, and to himself as well in the depths of his consciousness, William remained naggingly an American, and perhaps his passion for Walt Whitman's *Leaves of Grass* was evidence of this. Unlike most other expatriates he never lost or tried to lose his native accent, and he remained proud of New York City's tremendous vitality. He made several return visits to favorite places in the States—Gettysburg, the Massachusetts coast, the long stretch of the Hudson downriver from Albany—that he remembered from his boyhood.

From this secure office on Victoria Embankment, said H. G. Wells, who interviewed him there for his 1906 book, *The Future in America,* William Waldorf Astor drew "gold from New York"—perhaps $6 million a year in rents—"as effectually as a ferret draws blood from a rabbit." He commanded an empire of office buildings; immense apartment houses on upper Broadway; blocks of decaying but invariably profitable tenement properties; the northern half of the famous old Astor House, built by his great-grandfather and still doing business; the Waldorf half of the Waldorf-Astoria; and all of another hotel, the New Netherland, built to his specifications at a cost of about $3 million and, along with the Waldorf, opened in 1892. The *Times* welcomed the New Netherland as "the second of the magnificent creations of this sort which William Waldorf Astor has completed."

Seventeen stories high, promoted as the tallest hotel structure in the world and the first to have telephones in every room and its own telephone exchange, the New Netherland commanded the main entrance to Central Park at Fifty-ninth Street and Fifth Avenue. In external style a gabled and turreted brown brick version of German Renaissance architecture, his new hotel was similar to the Waldorf, but it had a a different ambience altogether, one of subdued but substantial elegance. In effect a marketplace and theater, the Waldorf-Astoria enclosed a world of glitter, wealth, and fashion bathed in an unremitting blaze of publicity. The New Netherland was aristocratic, reserved, and refined, more like a private club than a public facility. Reflecting William's distaste for what he felt was the vulgarity of American democracy and its army of journalists, the New Netherland, not the Waldorf-Astoria, was where he stayed on his occasional business visits to New York. Especially compared with the Waldorf, the New Netherland proved to be a financial disappointment and a managerial problem. At one point, embroiled in a bitter conflict with the resident "proprietor," General Ferdinand Earle, Astor evicted him and his family for nonpayment of back rent. He ordered the hotel emptied of its over two hundred guests, stripped of the furnishings installed by Earle, and briefly shut down. Even so, despite this experience, the New Netherland was not to be the last of Astor's innkeeping enterprises. For all his fastidiousness and snobbery he remained as passionate and knowing about luxury hotels for the American public as about Greco-Roman statuary and estates in the English countryside.

Even before 1899, when William finally renounced his citizenship to become a subject of Queen Victoria, his public career and conduct had become topics of outrage on both sides of the ocean. To his former countrymen he was a traitor who had fled to England like Benedict Arnold or Judah P. Benjamin, Jefferson Davis's secretary of state; an ingrate who unforgivably, for all his advantages, had managed to find life in America not good enough for him; a coward who slunk away from politics after failing even to buy elective office; a would-be leader of New York society who ceded the field to his aunt, *the* Mrs. Astor, and her feckless son Jack. Like a burglar with a sack of family plate and candlesticks over his shoulder, he was seen to be taking American dollars abroad and, in the hope of buying himself a title, liberally bestowing them on the British. He gave millions of dollars to British universities, hospitals, and charities, and to the British army (including a $25,000 artillery battery) during the Boer War and World War I.

Apart from the buildings in New York he had put up and the rents sweated from decaying slum properties there, Astor's wealth represented the unearned increment of Manhattan land bought for a few dollars by earlier generations of Astors and now worth many times more than what they had paid for them. The owners had done virtually nothing in the meantime to alleviate the misery and increase the value of their extensive tenement holdings beyond holding them. The Astors toiled not, neither did they spin, but an earthly father, free enterprise, and compound interest had endowed them with the glories of Solomon. The enormous surplus value vested in their property did not belong to the Astors, it could be said by single taxers, socialists, and other reform-minded thinkers of the era: it belonged to the sweated wage earners whose labors had turned a low-lying village on Manhattan Island into the de facto commercial capital of the United States. Manhattan's elevator-served, steel-framed office and residential buildings rose to the skies from their footings in the most expensive real estate in the world. William's departure from New York provoked, among other sendoffs from the press, a reference to his family's origins in "a German slaughterhouse" and derisive reminders of his unavailing efforts through hired genealogists to connect his beer-swilling forebears with "persons of condition" in the Crusades.

When the news of the ex-American's formal declaration of allegiance to Queen Victoria arrived by cable in New York, demonstrators cheered on by crowds of spectators erected and set fire to an oil-soaked life-size effigy of "William the Traitor" on the stretch of Broadway soon to be named Times Square. The police arrived and chased the crowd away, but not before the effigy had gone up in flames and left a smoking crater in the asphalt. W. W. ASTOR BECOMES A BRITISH SUBJECT: the *Times* ran the news on page one and pointedly juxtaposed it to an item about the military company the patriotic Colonel John Jacob Astor IV was raising to fight in the American war with Spain. William read these stories in the papers, put them in his scrapbook, pored over the clippings, and used them to stoke his undying fire of outrage at the American press.

To loyal Englishmen, William Waldorf Astor was their worst dream of an American invader who bought his way into society, bought (and rebuilt, often heedless of tradition, to suit his extravagant tastes) estates that were part of the nation's heritage, denied the public access to them, and also bought his way into journalism. "If this sort of thing is allowed to go on," one London journal complained, "we shall soon be governed, not by Downing [Street], but by Wall Street." He sent his sons to Eton and Oxford, and at a time when the United States was at war with Spain, and Jack Astor was rallying to the colors to see combat in Cuba, he entered the elder of the two, Waldorf, in Queen Victoria's Household Cavalry. William's money, purpose, and pride eventually prevailed over all the resistance and resentment he provoked. He could outspend, outcollect, outentertain, and outbuild anyone in England.

By 1897, when the combined Waldorf and Astoria hotels went into full operation and hosted the Bradley-Martin extravaganza, William had already established himself as being among London's premier hosts. That year one of his receptions and concert evenings at Carlton House Terrace counted among the guests the Grand Duke and Grand Duchess Michael of Russia, Prince Alexander of Teck, the lord lieutenant of Ireland, and, the papers reported, "a host of English dukes, earls, and counts, with their duchesses and countesses. . . . The display of jewels was simply prodigious, and the house was a mass of flowers." Two celebrities, the Australian soprano Nellie Melba and the Polish piano virtuoso Ignace Paderewski, were among the performing artists.

These glittering events, high points of the London social season, inevitably began to attract party crashers. Cursed with a low boiling point of indignation and a towering sense of lordship, William decided to do something about these affronts and make an example of the next interloper. "It angered me, perhaps unduly," he confessed to Amy Richardson long after the event, "that my house should be regarded as a place of public amusement. . . . I allowed my temper to carry me beyond the bounds of moderation."

Captain Sir Berkeley Milne, a distinguished British naval officer, arrived at a concert evening at Carlton House Terrace in July 1900. He escorted one of William's invited guests, Lady Orford. Unaware of the lady's sponsorship of Milne, William found an occasion to assert both principle and authority as host. He confronted the captain, refused to shake hands with him, and demanded to know his name. He then sent the captain packing with the promise that all of London would soon know of this infraction of good manners. The next day, still possessed by what he considered justifiable outrage, William published an item in his newspaper, the *Pall Mall Gazette*. "We are desired to make known that the presence of Captain Sir Berkeley Milne of the Naval and Military Club, Piccadilly, at Mr. Astor's concert last Thursday evening was uninvited."

William learned right away that he had kicked over a hornet's nest. Protégé and intimate of the Prince of Wales, Milne was the former commander of the royal yacht *Osborne*, a future admiral, and on all counts the wrong man to boot out of the party. Lady Orford and her friends responded to what was construed as an insult extending far beyond her injured sensibilities and those of Captain Milne to the entire British navy, from first lord of the admiralty to Jack Tar thirsting for his daily dipper of grog. Milne's patron, the Prince of Wales, reportedly regarded the incident as unpardonable and intended to have William ejected from the royal circle at Marlborough House. With all of London talking, even the aged queen, who had reigned for almost seventy years, was said to have "interested herself in the matter." William finally published a grudging apology in his paper, but it was a while before the dust settled. An affair of negligible specific gravity had mutated, if not into a tiny reprise of the War of 1812, at least into a farce that managed to make everyone look silly, especially its hot-tempered instigator. One noble earl called William "a purse-proud American, whose dollars could not save him from the contempt of his countrymen." Further incurring the royal wrath by snubbing Mrs. George Keppel, Edward's mistress ("a public strumpet"), William had to wait until 1916, by which time both Victoria and Edward VII were dead, before his wealth and strategically placed benefactions eased his way to the peerage.

"Congratulations are due to the English people, already pretty well occupied with many serious questions," a *New York Times* editorial commented on the Milne affair from across the Atlantic, "upon the breaking up of a storm center at home that threatened for a few moments to add to the worries of the English speaking and reading race. . . . We beg to renew to our British brethren the assurances of our continued sympathy and esteem. You may forgive; if you are magnanimous you will forget. You may do both, but do not send him back." That editorial, too, went into William's scrapbook.

ii.

WILLIAM WALDORF ASTOR'S grandest English acquisition was Cliveden, a 376-acre estate of spectacular gardens, lawns, and woodlands along a serpentine stretch of the Upper Thames, twenty-six miles from London. All the spectacular beauty of "England's green and pleasant land" seemed to have been concentrated, with jewel-like brilliance, in this one place in Buckinghamshire. In 1893 he had rented Cliveden for five months from its owner, the Duke of Westminster. At the expiration of the rental term he bought the place outright for a reported sum of $1.25 million, but not without a bitter dispute with the duke over ownership of the visitors book that contained signatures going back to the seventeenth century. The great estate, and the history that came with it, satisfied Astor's seigneurial imagination and gave a transplanted American at least a probationary place in the English tradition. The original Cliveden main house had been built in 1666 by the Duke of Buckingham, a sometime favorite of King Charles II and famously satirized by poet laureate John Dryden:

Stiff in opinions, always in the wrong;
Was everything by starts, and nothing long:
But in the course of one revolving moon,
Was chemist, fiddler, statesman, and buffoon.

In a duel there, Buckingham killed his mistress's husband, the Earl of Shrewsbury. Cliveden had also been the residence of a British military hero, the Earl of Orkney, and of Frederick, Prince of Wales, father of George III. The composer Thomas Arne had his "Rule, Britannia" performed for the first time at Cliveden in 1740, about fifty years before the original house burned down. Sir Charles Barry, architect of the Houses of Parliament, replaced it with a baroque-style building that had a certain dominating and chilly grandeur but none of the esprit of the water tower, with a gilded clock face, that looked out over the entire estate. Queen Victoria had visited eight times. "It is a perfection of a place," she wrote in her journal, "first of all the view is so beautiful, & then the house is a bijou of taste." Cliveden had royal, aristocratic, and historical associations enough for the scholar, antiquarian, collector, and Anglophile in Astor. He was a time traveler like his cousin Jack, but his destination was a past securely in the grip of the old order.

Applying his educated taste in architecture and landscape, William set out to rescue Cliveden from what he charged was "the neglect and abandonment into which that dreadful old creature, the Duke of Westminster, had allowed it to sink." He took out of storage in Rome the immense stone balustrade from the Villa Borghese garden that he had bought years earlier during his tenure as U.S. ambassador and installed it below the house. His collection of Roman sarcophagi and funerary urns found a resting place on the great lawn. He also installed an ancient mosaic floor and a grand staircase in the main hall. For the dining room he ordered an ornate ceiling, painted under his supervision; a suite of eighteenth-century gilt wall paneling; and a table and other principal furniture that, along with the paneling, had once belonged to Madame de Pompadour. To face the front entrance of the house, about mid-way on the grand avenue from the main gate, he commissioned Thomas Waldo Story, son of the renowned sculptor William Wetmore Story and himself a favorite in Britain, to create the alarmingly large white-marble-and-volcanic-rock *Fountain of Love*. Writhing nudes disported themselves atop a giant scallop shell. "The female figures," Astor wrote in an interpretive note on the composition, "are supposed to have discovered the fountain of love, and to be experiencing the effects of its wonderful elixir." His taste in sculpture and painting remained as stubbornly antimodern as his politics and his devotion to the England of absolute monarchy. Bringing his life full circle, he moved into the Cliveden rose garden his *Wounded Amazon,* the statue, admired by George Templeton Strong, that he had made in his twenties, before duty to his father compelled him to put aside art in favor of real estate. Looking ahead, in a similar gesture of closure, he designed a resting place for his ashes in Cliveden's Octagon Temple, an eighteenth-century architectural conceit with a commanding view of the countryside and the winding Thames below. The structure had originally been a summer house; he had it made into a high church family chapel with an altar, a domed ceiling, and glass mosaics depicting the Annunciation, the Temptation of Eve, and scenes from the life of Christ.

For a century before William became its master, Cliveden had been open to visitors and sightseers, one of several showplaces in England that were in effect, and by long tradition, public parks maintained at private expense. The new owner enclosed Cliveden within a high wall topped with broken glass, forbade access to a spring of water that had been a local pleasure site, and erected a blank wall to replace the iron grille gate that had allowed a sweeping view up the long driveway leading to the forecourt of the house. By his order, boating parties were forbidden to land and picnic on Cliveden's riverbanks. Unlike neighboring estates in the Thames Valley, Cliveden was now closed to the public, evidence, as it was seen by indignant neighbors, of the arrogance of a rich American who scorned local custom and good manners and asserted his right to privacy at any cost. When in residence Astor had his personal flag with armorial bearings raised over the main house at 9 a.m. and lowered at sundown. "Cliveden was a court," his grandson, Michael Astor, recalled, "ruled over with a majestic sense of justice by a lonely autocrat who was obsessed by highly personal notions about convention. Everything in the house ran exactly to time. William Waldorf had a mania about punctuality." He demanded from his guests inflexible conformity to schedule, decreeing, for example, precisely when they should write their letters, stroll about the grounds, or ride into the village. On his orders the clocks at Cliveden were set an hour behind English summer time, a recent reform that he considered silly. A cartoonist in a London newspaper renamed Cliveden "Walled-off Astoria" and depicted its owner as a strutting eagle, a British flag tied to his tail, standing on a ground covered with bags of dollars. A sign, TRESPASSERS WILL BE PROSECUTED, hung on the by-now famous glass-studded wall. The cartoon showed William's twenty-one-year-old son, Waldorf, dressed in his Household Guards uniform, doing sentry duty on the battlements.

One of William Waldorf Astor's never-ending battles with the press took the form of a $5,000 libel suit against the *London Daily Mail*. Citing him as the source, the paper had published a frivolous article, headlined MR. ASTOR'S STRANGE DINNER PARTY: allegedly, he had bet a certain General Owen Williams $2,500 that the trunks of some California redwood trees were large enough when sliced transversely to make a table around which two dozen and more people could dine in comfort. To win the bet, the story went on, Astor ordered a sequoia slab sawed to his order in California, had it shipped to Cliveden, and there, on his new table under a tent on the grounds, he served an elegant dinner to the general and twenty-four other guests and won his bet. At worst this was just another mildly satiric tale about rich Americans—Kentucky colonels, Montana cattle barons, Chicago meat packers, Pittsburgh steel masters, California railroad magnates—who were often caricatured as braggarts trumpeting the wonders of their country while proudly infesting England's castles and stately homes.

Already fancying himself as British as any duke and with as much dignity to maintain, William wrote a heated letter to the *London Times* accusing the *Daily Mail* of libeling him as "a foolish and ridiculous person" by publishing "a deliberate and mischievous fabrication." He testified to that effect in open court before the lord chief justice. Through his distinguished counsel, formerly the queen's solicitor general, Astor complained that from time to time since settling in England he had been the subject of similar "personal and offensive paragraphs." The aftermath of the suit that he brought was as demeaning as that of his injudicious ouster of Captain Milne. Hearing the case, the lord chief justice had some fun at Astor's expense and, contrary to customary decorum, even invited raucous laughter in the courtroom. He himself had been the butt of such American-style pleasantries, his lordship said. He cited a London newspaper story to the effect that as president of the divorce court he himself had pronounced his own divorce from his wife. "We are not divorced," he said, "and I am not the president of the divorce court." He suggested that Mr. Astor, who (as everyone knew) had enjoyed similar experiences with the press back home in the States, should by now have been hardened to such nonsense. Advised by counsel against letting his grievance go to a jury, Astor accepted an apology from the *Daily Mail* and withdrew from legal combat. While it lasted, "the W. W. Astor Libel Suit," another chapter in the misadventures of a transplanted American Croesus, made good copy in both England and the States.

In 1906, having rescued Cliveden from decay and restored it to his exacting taste, Astor turned his drive to build and indulge his historical imagination to an even larger and more expensive enterprise than Cliveden. Mogul emperor Shah Jahan, builder of the Taj Mahal, and mad King Ludwig of Bavaria, builder of fantastic castles along the Danube, would have recognized the impulse. William bought Hever, a manor house estate in Kent, southeast of London. Once the childhood home of Anne Boleyn, second wife of Henry VIII, it later passed into the hands of Henry's fourth wife, Anne of Cleves. William spent four years and an estimated $10 million to make Hever conform to his historical imaginings and, in effect, regress it four hundred years. He had a surrounding ditch excavated into a moat and filled with water, built a new drawbridge and portcullis, and repaired the battlements. Hever now had a deer park, fountains, a boating lake, and, among modern improvements, a power-generating plant and waterworks.

At one point Astor employed 840 workmen of all trades inside and out to create for him, in the heart of twentieth-century England, a self-sustaining and self-contained medieval domain. Guarded by a wall twelve feet high, its 640 acres comprised a model farm; a 50-acre man-made lake, in spots sixteen feet deep, dug out of marsh and meadowland; two bridges to span the winding river that ran through the estate; newly planted forests; a deer park; walled gardens and a fountain; and barbered grounds surrounding a maze of yew hedge. To houseguests, servants, and estate workers Astor built an entire thatched-roof Tudor village separated from the castle by the moat, drawbridge, and double portcullis. An eight-man security force patrolled the gates and kept out automobiles, uninvited visitors, cameras, and especially the press. A poster at the local railway station informed the public that Hever, long one of the local attractions, was no longer open to visitors.

In an article Astor commissioned and published in his *Pall Mall Magazine* the writer, Olive Sebright, described Hever in terms that explain part of its appeal to the new owner. Hever was "a haunt of ancient peace," she wrote. "When we cross the bridge and pass under the double portcullis, we leave the world of to-day behind us, and in the old half-timbered courtyard, lose all sense of surprise and speculation. Life becomes a dream of tranquil simplicity, and the fitness of it all fills and satisfies our restless spirit." Lordship of Hever Castle, surrounded there by artifacts of an era of absolute monarchy, gave Astor not only a private retreat from the present but a solitude in which to enjoy his treasures and the illusion of living in another time.

He dwelled alone in the ancient manor house that he had converted into a one-bedroom medieval castle furnished with skillfully adapted modern conveniences such as indoor plumbing and electricity. However anachronistic, he made such comforts the dominant note in his bedroom. "I should not like to live in a museum," he told Amy Richardson.

DRAWBRIDGE RISES FOR ASTOR ENTRY: newspapers ridiculed his improvements and accused him of "ruining" Hever just as (in their view) he had ruined Cliveden. But, just as he had done at Cliveden, he imposed his will and wealth on his property. When in residence at Hever Castle he flew his personal flag over the battlements. It displayed the coat of arms that supposedly linked the Astor butchers and rabbit skinners to a Franco-Spanish line of noble descent going back to the Crusades. He furnished Hever's great hall and minstrels' gallery with shields, banners, tapestries, pennants, halberds, swords, suits of armor, instruments of torture and punishment, and vanloads of museum pieces from the shops and warehouses of Regent Street and Bond Street dealers in antiquities. Established in such surroundings he enjoyed the prospect of one day entering the peerage as Baron (later Viscount) Astor of Hever Castle. Through agents and advisers he assembled a notable art collection at Hever that rivaled Henry Clay Frick's in New York: it included Holbein's portraits of Henry VIII and Anne Boleyn, Titian's Philip II, Clouet's Edward VI, and Cranach's Martin Luther. He liked to believe that Hever was haunted by the ghost of Anne Boleyn, sent to the headsman's block by her husband, who accused her of incest and adultery. Her prayer book and bed were among the relics Astor acquired and installed at Hever. According to local legend, the headless queen, accompanied by a headless black dog, nightly walked the castle's dark passageways and windswept battlements. Making an exception to his ban on allowing strangers to penetrate his feudal fastness, Astor invited ghost hunters from the British Society for Psychical Research to keep a vigil at Hever. They reported no sightings.

iii.

WHILE WILLIAM WALDORF ASTOR completed his transformation into an Englishman of the highest rank, his patriotic cousin Jack entered upon a military career of sorts. It had had its beginnings in 1894 with a largely ceremonial appointment. Jack's Rhinecliff neighbor New York governor-elect Levi P. Morton, a Republican banker who had been Benjamin Harrison's vice president, chose Jack, and half a dozen other rich and socially prominent civilians, to serve on his military staff as aides-de-camp. This granted Jack the rank of colonel, the duty of escorting the governor on public occasions, and the right to carry a sword and wear a gold-braid aiguillette on a dress uniform tailored for him at great expense.

Jack's appointment to a position of honor and display rather than valor and discipline did little to redeem his reputation from years of providing entertainment for newspaper and gossip-sheet readers. But he was soon in harmony with the war fever against Spain that was to sweep the United States. He had firm and outspoken convictions about the destiny of Cuba, which, he believed, was to be liberated from the grip of Spain and annexed to the

United States. With the destruction of the battleship *Maine* in Havana Harbor in February 1898, the idea of a war with Spain came to a boil in the minds of President William McKinley, Secretary of State John Hay, Assistant Secretary of the Navy Theodore Roosevelt, and newspaper publisher William Randolph Hearst. Jack moved with purpose and vigor to win for himself a place in the army. He wished to be "Colonel Astor" as fervently as William wished to be "Viscount Astor." Putting aside his normally unshakable Astor pride, he lobbied, wheedled, and politicked in Washington, applied pressure and influence in the right quarters, and, in effect, engineered for himself a commission as army inspector general with the rank of lieutenant colonel. His appointment to the volunteer army, the *Times* noted dourly, had been made "without relevancy to the good of the service." The notion of Jack Astor strapping on a sword and mounting a neighing battle steed aroused hilarity in the general public as well as resentment among more qualified warriors who were also seeking a commission.

Mr. Dooley, satirist Finley Peter Dunne's fictional Irish saloon philosopher, had Jack and his ilk in mind when he announced his views of the war in a nationally circulated column in the *Chicago Journal*. Mr. Dooley depicted a freshly minted officer in mufti, wearing an English suit and accompanied by his valet, as he explained to President McKinley why he was unable to leave immediately for the front in Cuba: "Me pink silk pijammas hasn't arrived." "Wait f'r th' pijammas," McKinley tells this would-be Alexander the Great. "Thin on to war . . . an' let ye'er watchword be, 'Raymimber ye'er manners.' " Dooley predicted, "We'll put th' tastiest ar-rmy in th' field that iver came out of a millinery shop." Special correspondents from *Butterick's Patterns* and *Harper's*

Bazaar, he said, would soon be following onto the field of combat in Cuba the most fashionably dressed military force that ever creased its pants.

Jack gave good value for his appointment. He lent the navy his refurbished 250-foot, 745-ton yacht *Nourmahal* and offered free passage for troops and volunteers on his Illinois Central Railroad. He raised, equipped, and trained at his own expense—$75,000 and much more, as needed—the Astor Battery, a regiment of mountain artillery for service in Cuba and the Philippines: six rapid-firing Hotchkiss field guns served by 102 enlisted men with the words "Astor Battery" stamped in gold letters on uniforms, hats, and knapsacks. Brass buttons on their tunics bore the letter A and an eagle. Jack accompanied his Astor Battery to Cuba. Himself properly kitted out in field uniform and campaign hat, and with binoculars slung around his neck, Astor stood with the artist Frederic Remington within rifle and artillery range of the Spanish fortifications on San Juan Hill. Before they were ordered to move out of "this hellspot," as Remington called it, they witnessed the uphill charge that was in effect Rough Rider colonel Theodore Roosevelt's dramatic first step toward the presidency.

Jack returned from a month in Cuba unscathed except for a touch of fever contracted in the field (and a shrapnel wound to his horse). On furlough after delivering dispatches to the War Department, he was reported to be planning to rejoin the army and his Astor Battery in the Philippines. An accompanying news item reported that the *Nourmahal,* back in its owner's hands after uneventful service with the navy, had remained true to form: it had run hard and fast aground in the Hudson off Haverstraw, some twenty-five miles downriver from Ferncliff.

For the rest of his life, and posthumously as well, Jack was

"Colonel Astor," patriot, war hero, and gallant gentleman. He had stood "ready to answer any call his country may make upon him," as he told a reporter from the *New York Times,* and he was outspoken in his scorn for his renegade cousin William Waldorf Astor. He even played the genealogical card against his cousin. Unlike William, he could cite descent on his mother's side from patriots of the Revolutionary period. "I have the blood in me of my grandmother, who was a sister of Colonel Henry Armstrong and a daughter of General Armstrong. They were both true Americans and the Armstrong blood is strong in me." Although somewhat eroded by his exemplary war service, Jack's old reputation as playboy and dilettante remained nearly impossible to shake. When the Murray Hill Republican Club proposed him for Congress (on a ticket with Colonel Theodore Roosevelt as governor), Tammany boss Richard Croker effectively shot down the idea. "I will stick to it that Astor is an ass," he declared. "And that an ass even though an Astor has no business in the Congress of the United States."

With no position in the Congress or any other public body, the demobilized warrior devoted his energies to Caribbean cruises aboard the *Nourmahal,* his collection of about sixty motorcars, his laboratory and workshop, his stable of Thoroughbreds, and two principal residences: Ferncliff, one of the largest country estates in America; and 840–842 Fifth Avenue, the white marble double mansion he shared with his mother. He belonged to more than forty clubs in New York, Tuxedo, Newport, Paris, and London. European travel, visits to Palm Beach, and, for shooting, to Aiken, South Carolina, were among other pleasures and distractions in what was generally recognized as a life without a significant focus aside from the mainly titular management of his business interests.

As head of the American branch of the Astor estate he controlled immense business and residential realty holdings all over Manhattan, including his half of the Waldorf-Astoria and the old Astor House. He had a seat on the boards of the Delaware and Hudson Railroad, the Illinois Central Railroad, New York Life Insurance, Niagara Falls Power, Western Union Telegraph, several banks, and at least a dozen other companies. Fast trains between Albany and New York City made special stops for him at Rhinecliff to accommodate his business trips to the Astor estate office on West Twenty-sixth Street.

Together with eighty-five other "representative men," in 1905 Colonel John Jacob Astor was a subject of virtual canonization in a mammoth (twelve-by-eighteen-inch) gilt-edged, opulently bound and illustrated album, offered to subscribers at $1,500 a copy: *Fads and Fancies: Representative Americans at the Beginning of the Twentieth Century, Being a Portrayal of Their Tastes, Diversions, and Achievements.* The creator of this ultimate vanity book was the longtime gossip journalist and shakedown artist Colonel William D'Alton Mann, publisher of *Town Topics.* With *Fads and Fancies,* a grotesquely mild title for a hagiography of American capitalists and firebooters, Colonel Mann hoped to cash in on a lifetime of work.

Some of the subscribers the colonel recruited were agreeable to having considerably more than the nominal $1,500 extracted from them as the price of admission to his hall of heroes. The widow of railroad builder and robber baron Collis P. Huntington, for instance, insisted that her husband deserved a more ample treatment in *Fads and Fancies* than relative nobodies such as match manufacturer Ohio C. Barber; Isaac F. Emerson, a former drug-store clerk who invented Bromo-Seltzer; society sportsman Foxhall Keene; and asphalt millionaire A. L. Barber. She paid $10,000 for eight pages instead of the meager three or four allotted to other eminent corporate operators like Thomas W. Lawson, Boston stock plunger, market manipulator, and author of *Frenzied Finance;* traction magnate and convicted embezzler Charles T. Yerkes, whose "ruling passion" was his love of "all beautiful things," especially rugs and tapestries; Julius Fleischmann of Cincinnati, heir to the family yeast and vinegar works; and Reginald "Reggie" Vanderbilt, boozer and man about town, whose great-grandfather, the implacable Commodore, was credited in passing with having radiated "pure sunshine in his life and character." ("I won't sue you, for the law is too slow," Vanderbilt once told a former business associate. "I'll ruin you.")

Given four pages, Colonel John Jacob Astor was among the more conspicuous of the men immortalized in the folio pages of *Fads and Fancies*. He clearly cooperated with the publisher and contributed a dozen or so pictures from private albums to go with his write-up. Among them were photos of himself in civilian clothes and in military uniform, armed with a cavalry saber and mounted on his horse. Other pictures displayed his yacht and launches; his Ferncliff mansion, gatehouse, and tennis court; one of his automobiles; and the battery of howitzers he had given to the U.S. Army.

"Of the typical American gentlemen of the first years of the Twentieth Century," Jack's chapter began,

> the "Master of Ferncliff" affords as admirable an example as a wide knowledge of men and the times can choose. Born with the proverbial silver spoon, yet inheriting the tastes of the scholar and the traveler rather than that of the Sybarite, together with a strong but bravely tolerant patriotism, his equipment for the role was at once liberal and promising. In his country's recent conquests in the West Indies and the

South Pacific he has played a worthy part, and his personal services, as well as his riches, were placed at his nation's command in her time of need.

In his ability to combine recreation with a painstaking attention to the many duties that of necessity devolve upon the conscientious man of millions, Colonel Astor possesses a rare and valuable gift. To the average observer he must appear as a gentleman of careless leisure; nevertheless, Colonel Astor personally oversees the conduct of the Astor estate in every particular. Clear-headed and keen-witted, no detail escapes him. Surrounded by capable lieutenants who have been trained to his methods, he has reduced this labor to a matter of a few hours a day in a few days of the year.

Among the colonel's recent ventures with claims on his attention during these few business hours had been two new hotels in midtown Manhattan.

EIGHT

"Mine! All Mine!"

i.

IN SEPTEMBER 1904, after an absence of five years, William Waldorf Astor, at fifty-six, vigorous and ruddy in face, arrived in New York on the steamship *Majestic* for a short visit. He was accompanied by a valet and seventeen pieces of luggage and went directly to his suite at the New Netherland. Having been burned in effigy in his native city some years earlier, it was with some reluctance that he had left the Tudor world of Hever Castle in the hands of its putative ghost and its army of workmen. He came back to tend to business affairs, chief among them the opening of the Astor, his new luxury hotel at Times Square. A month later his cousin, John Jacob Astor IV, was also to open an ambitious new hotel of his own. Jack's was the St. Regis, and he intended it to exceed all others, including William's, in luxury, modernity, and the smartness of its clientele. Meanwhile the Waldorf-Astoria, their joint venture, continued to prosper, although the tide of fashion and commerce was moving uptown.

Despite his ingrained resentment of the American press, William Waldorf Astor managed to be affable and even forthcoming in conversation with reporters who boarded the ship at quarantine. They were surprised that despite his long residence in England, he sounded as if he had never left Manhattan. So far from selling off his real-estate holdings there, as had been widely rumored, he assured reporters that he was continuing to add to them, the Hotel Astor being his newest acquisition and, as it turned out, the last of his grand gestures on Manhattan Island.

He had committed about $7 million to the building of a brick-and-limestone hotel, to stand twelve stories high and occupy an entire block front in Longacre Square, on the west side of Broadway between Forty-fourth and Forty-fifth streets. In April, five months before his return, Longacre Square, the city's tourist and entertainment hub, had been renamed Times Square. The name recognized the newspaper's rising new headquarters at Forty-second Street, a New World version of Giotto's Florentine bell tower. Twenty-two stories when completed, it was the tallest building in midtown. In its basement, above the pressroom on lower levels, was the Times Square station of financier August Belmont's newly completed Interborough Rapid Transit Company. For a nickel, subway riders could now travel from City Hall to 145th Street and Broadway in fifteen minutes. Along with the Times Tower, the Hotel Astor stood at a critical junction—"The Crossroads of the World"—of foot, surface, and underground traffic flowing north, south, and crosstown. Ablaze with spectacular electrical advertising signs, the city's entertainment and tourist center had already been dubbed the Great White Way and was soon to become as famous a focus of public assembly as London's Piccadilly Circus and the Vatican's St. Peter's Square.

In making this brilliantly timed and strategically situated investment, Astor had followed the advice of a German-born restaurateur, owner of a popular eatery and gathering place nearby called the Arena, William C. Muschenheim. Once manager of the cadets' mess at West Point, he was an old hand at dispensing loaves and fishes and made a great deal of money at it. Scholar, art lover, and enthusiastic local historian, he owned a notable collection of old New York maps, documents, and prints. He had a sure sense of where the future lay. In the course of his correspondence with Astor and his occasional visits to England he had made a strong case for the claim that Times Square, an increasingly populous stretch of the city's most celebrated area, needed, and would amply support, a fittingly great hotel that should be as renowned for its food, drink, and congenial atmosphere as for its accommodations and architectural splendor. This new hotel was to be an updated version of the Waldorf-Astoria, an equally monumental and decisive venture, but in spirit less snooty, more egalitarian, and more in tune with the commercial values and increasingly relaxed social style of the new American century. Instead of the exotics of high society, its core clientele was to be tourists, businesspeople, and prosperous members of the middle class.

Astor and Muschenheim gave their designers, decorators, engineers, and purchasing agents free rein and a virtually unlimited budget. Their architects, Clinton and Russell, until then mainly known for designing tall business buildings, tore down a shabby block of shops, theatrical boardinghouses, and saloons to provide the site for a new palace for the people. From its wine cellar, two stories below street level, to its roof garden, observatory, belvedere restaurant, and cavernous ballrooms under the mansard roof, the Astor, promoted to the public as "the finest hotel in the world," was to be "far more than a stopping place": a self-sufficient, self-enclosed magic city within a city. Muschenheim's exuberant prose hailed the Astor as "the Culmination of Years of Artistic Study." The cutaway view that he commissioned as an advertisement suggests a combination of industrial plant and bustling ant farm.

"In New York," his lavishly illustrated promotional booklet declared, "the hotel of ten years ago has undergone an amazing evolution—an evolution which has now produced one of the most magnificent and brilliant factors of modern life. Here has grown up an institution new in the world—a phenomenon—a development of which a decade ago we did not dream, and which the capitals of Europe are only beginning to copy."

Covering fourteen building lots, the Astor enclosed a vast marble and gilded lobby twenty-one feet high, decorated with murals depicting New York past and present. Almost immediately the lobby became the equivalent of a municipal living room, agora, and trysting place. "She Lost It at the Astor" was a popular song of the 1930s. "Meet me at the Astor" became part of the social vocabulary of well-heeled New Yorkers. Upstairs were more than five hundred bedrooms served by twelve passenger elevators, a banqueting hall seating five hundred, a thirty-five-thousand-square-foot kitchen described as the largest in the world, dozens of public rooms, each with its own distinct character, and guest suites that drew on a lexicon of styles—art nouveau, Empire, Dutch Renaissance—and made inevitable references to Versailles. Some of the Astor's technological innovations were air-conditioning; fire and smoke detectors in every room; electrically controlled fire doors; a "food escalator" connecting the kitchen and banqueting rooms; an ice plant that produced 120 tons each day; an array of dynamos powering the elevators and the hotel's fourteen thousand lights; and a "crematory," or incinerator, the first of its kind in a hotel, to dispose of trash and garbage. From a glassed-in basement enclosure that protected them from heat and noise, hotel guests, as if they were visiting the innards of an ocean liner, could look out over the engines and boilers that served this gargantuan machine for living. The Astor's interior and exterior walls were fortresslike in thickness and strength.

A carnival of cosmopolitanism, the Astor housed an American Indian grill room; a Chinese tearoom; a Flemish smoking room; a Spanish lounging room; a Pompeian billiard room; a German "Hunt Room" decorated with stag-horn light fixtures and a continuous frieze showing scenes of the chase; and a Mediterranean orangery complete with fountain, a grove of fruit trees and palms, and an electrically lit moon that shed a warm romantic glow on the occupants. Private dining rooms on the ninth floor were fitted out as the cabin of a millionaire's yacht; paintings shaped and framed like portholes depicted the waterway between the harbor and Long Island Sound and created the illusion that diners had embarked on a leisurely cruise out of the city. Muschenheim's pet project, the American Indian Grill Room, was an ethnological museum of sorts furnished with bows and arrows, feathered headdresses, baskets, ritual artifacts, hunting and fishing implements, busts, rare prints, and photographs. Some of this material had been assembled with advice from the American Museum of Natural History. The Astor's "hall of the aborigines" was to serve as a reminder to diners, the management announced, that "the wigwam of the Indian once stood on the very ground now occupied by our great cities."

Although lord of Cliveden and Hever Castle, William Waldorf Astor had no hesitation about dining in public view at this unashamedly commercial and democratic hotel and allowing it to bear the family name. Himself an appreciative feeder and wine drinker, he was delighted with the Astor cuisine, which he claimed was the best in New York. Muschenheim's encyclopedic menus of-fered rare dishes like wild boar, English snipe, and Egyptian quail. Astor admitted to some slight unease when he saw that the hotel chinaware bore a prominent design of flowering asters. "I am not responsible for the use of the China Aster as a joke upon my name," he told Amy Richardson. "Muschenheim hit upon the idea and was delighted with it." The new hotel proved to be so success-ful that in 1906, less than two years after it opened, Astor invested a further $4 million. He doubled the building's size by extending it to the west, added the Astor Theater on the corner of Forty-fifth Street, and topped the entire structure with the world's largest roof garden. The Astor's guest book eventually contained the names of practically every hero and famous person of the era. Among them were transatlantic solo flier Charles A. Lindbergh; General John J. Pershing, commander of the American Expeditionary Force in World War I; and the humorist Will Rogers. Republican presiden-tial candidate Charles Evans Hughes went to bed at the Astor on election night, 1916, believing he had defeated Woodrow Wilson. He woke up the next morning, after the returns from California had come in, to be told by a reporter he was "no longer president."

Despite the triumph of his new venture, Astor's mood turned glum after a few days of what he complained had been the cus-tomary "notoriety, abuse, and ridicule" he received at the hands of the local press. His stay "would have been pleasanter," he said, "had the newspaper men not dogged me about and Kodak-ed me with such patient industry." His enormous American-derived wealth combined with his declared allegiance to the British Crown had made him both a curiosity and a notoriety, subject of the in-evitable references to Benedict Arnold and to the rabbit skinner in the Astors' ancestry. As he had on previous occasions, he vowed "never to set foot in New York again."

ii.

FOLLOWING his cousin's example, John Jacob Astor IV also built in Times Square, on the southeast corner of Broadway and Forty-second Street. His Hotel Knickerbocker, opened in 1906 after construction costs of about $3.5 million, stood on one of the most valuable pieces of land in his Manhattan Island holdings, but, compared to the Astor, it was relatively low-key in decor and amenities and positioned in the hotel market to draw out-of-town visitors of moderate means. The management promised Fifth Avenue comforts at Broadway prices. Despite the fame of its barroom adorned with the popular artist Maxfield Parrish's mural *Old King Cole and His Fiddlers Three,* the Knickerbocker was never a success, and Prohibition finished it off. (The *Old King Cole* mural was moved uptown and installed in the St. Regis.)

Much closer to Jack Astor's heart and technological interests was his St. Regis, opened in 1904 a month or so after his cousin's Astor. It was a direct challenge to William's imperial style and asserted Jack's own personality, chronically undervalued but now enhanced by his public identity as Colonel Astor. Suggesting a decidedly masculine sort of competition, the new St. Regis was one story higher than the vaunted seventeen of William's New Netherland. The $6 million hotel Jack Astor erected on the southeast corner of Fifth Avenue and Fifty-fifth Street was acknowledged right away to be the last word in the design, furnishings, and technology of "a great modern American hotel," wrote Arthur C.

David, a critic for *Architectural Record*. In the grip of an apparent paroxysm of wonderment, he went on to describe the St. Regis (named after a resort area in upstate New York) as an example of "probably the most complicated piece of mechanism which the invention and ingenuity of man have ever been called upon to devise. The only other modern mechanical contrivances which might be in the same class are a contemporary battleship and ocean-liner; and in some respects the requirements of a hotel are more numerous and various than those even of a steamship of the highest class. . . . The bowels and frame of such a building are in truth comparable only to the human body in the complexity and interdependence of the processes that go on within."

Unlike the frankly egalitarian Hotel Astor in Times Square, the St. Regis was located in what had become known as "Vanderbilt Alley," a neighborhood of mansions, town houses, exclusive clubs, and high-end retail establishments like Cartier that catered to society and the very rich. It implicitly defined its clientele as the smart set: moneyed, luxury-loving, fastidious but elegantly casual, harbingers of an era of plush nightclubs, café society, and a general loosening of old-line social and sexual conventions. Inevitably, given the modernity of its presiding spirit, Jack's St. Regis began to draw younger patrons away from the old (by Manhattan standards) Waldorf-Astoria. Jack's passion for invention and innovation was visible in the hotel's air-conditioning and forced-air ventilation system, thermostats and telephones in every room, and mail chutes on each floor by the banks of bronze-doored elevators. Normally aloof from her husband and his interests, Ava reportedly had a hand in designing some of the period interiors.

Whatever guests required in the way of convenience, comfort, novelty, and visual splendor, Jack's new hotel offered them, including a library of leather-bound books, an "Elizabethan" tearoom hung with Flemish tapestries depicting incidents in the life of King Solomon, a sidewalk café, a skylight ballroom on the eighteenth floor, and a bronze-and-glass sentry box for the doorman. In the immense dining room, modeled on the Hall of Mirrors at Versailles, Harry Lehr's wife was able to give a party for 150 guests. She seated all of them at one table that was so long, she recalled, that in laying out the hotel's silver, Royal Worcester china, crystal, and linen, the waiters had to telephone "directions from one end of the table to another; while the florist's men, in special shoes of white felt, walked about on the surface of the table to arrange their trails of roses and carnations."

Within a month of its opening the St. Regis had generated so much press coverage all over the country that the resident lessee, a Hungarian named R. M. Haan, said he had no need to advertise. He believed, however, that many potential guests had been frightened away by the extravagance of some of the claims that had been made for his hotel. Satiric items in the comic papers speculated about how it might feel to sleep in a museum-quality bed that supposedly had cost the hotel owners $10,000, or to pay $500 for a half portion of chocolate éclair. "There has been the wildest exaggeration about my prices," Haan told a reporter. "They are slightly higher but not alarmingly so. The difference is in the service, china, and the objects of art and refined luxury in my dining room. My hotel is not a place for billionaires only, but a hostelry for people of good taste who have the means to live as comfortably as they choose."

Between them, and in competition with each other, but with William setting the pace, the incompatible Astor cousins built about half a dozen hotels, three of which were triumphantly popular and profitable ventures that shaped the face and style of New York. By inheritance and long-standing policy as New York's landlords and slumlords, the two Astors made themselves their city's premier innkeepers, and in so doing they virtually invented the American luxury hotel. What motivated them was not mere hope of gain: the entire landscape of venture and acquisition capitalism had been open to them as heirs of the first John Jacob Astor. They could have made more money just by doing nothing but raking in rents, interest, and dividends from what they already owned. They had chosen hotels to be the stage for a family drama of pride, spite, rivalry, self-projection, and the love of grandeur and prominence. A visitor from abroad imagined these "amazing Astors" strolling along Broadway and Fifth Avenue, stretching their arms to point, and exclaiming, "Mine! Mine! All mine!"

iii.

AFTER NEARLY three years of seclusion following a stroke, *the* Mrs. Astor—née Caroline Webster Schermerhorn—died in October 1908 at the age of seventy-eight. She left her famous diamonds to her son along with a five-strand pearl necklace that the appraisers found also held ninety imitation stones. In her last years she had withdrawn into a sweet and harmless fantasy, abetted by her servants and attendant nurses, that she was still living in her glory days. A month before she died, in a flash of hypomania she overcame her lifelong reluctance to grant interviews. "I can speak with authority about our young people," she said, referring to women who "smoke and drink and do other terrible things."

"They are of a new age and have ideas different from my conservative ones. . . . I am not vain enough to think New York will not be able to get along very well without me."

Edith Wharton's short story "After Holbein" pictures Mrs. Astor at the end of her life, "a poor old lady gently dying of softening of the brain" and imagining herself still "New York's leading hostess." Wearing her purple-black wig, she receives a stream of imaginary guests in her grand house on Fifth Avenue, an "entertaining machine" that dispensed terrapin, canvasback ducks, saddles of mutton and legs of lamb, magnums of champagne, and pyramids of hothouse fruit "to the same faces, perpetually the same faces, gathered stolidly about the same gold plate." "She had lived, breathed, invested and reinvested her millions to no other end."

Queen Victoria's death seven years earlier, said H. G. Wells, had been like the removal of "a great paper-weight that for half a century sat upon men's minds." Mrs. Astor's demise was comparably liberating. For two or three decades, much as Victoria had presided over her empire and her household, Mrs. Astor had presided over New York "society" and its inner group, the so-called Four Hundred. She favored the old colonial and Knickerbocker families, Schermerhorns and Armstrongs, from whom she was descended, and she looked down on relative newcomers such as the Vanderbilts. During her reign Caroline Astor imposed principles of decorum on a self-appointed American aristocracy that was founded on descent, inherited money, and a code of exclusion but on no discernible intrinsic merit such as intellect, learning, or originality. She had been a one-woman regulatory agency like the Interstate Commerce Commission, established in the same era to impose a comparable order on business. "Society," in the sense Caroline Astor defined and institutionalized it, did not altogether die with her, but like a spray of her hothouse orchids struck by frost, it shriveled. Outside of the surviving members of the Four Hundred, their offspring, and their imitators, hardly anyone of sense in the larger world missed it or mourned it.

Caroline's son, John Jacob Astor IV, was among those liberated by her departure. With his family, he had been living in the white marble double mansion at 840–842 Fifth Avenue that for years had been Caroline's residence as well and the setting for her famously selective and glittering dances and dinners. Although shackled in marriage to each other, he and the beautiful Ava were thoroughly alienated and rarely seen together, even on the same continent at the same time. A daughter, Alice, had been born to them in 1902, more than ten years after their marriage in 1891 and the birth of their son Vincent, but this had apparently only aggravated rather than eased the tensions between them; moreover, the child was rumored not to be Jack's. Their options had been limited. In the eyes of faithful High Church Episcopalians such as the Astors, mother and son, divorce was a sin and, conceivably, something worse, an embarrassment, because it violated the sanctity of the wedding vow by demanding, as New York State law then did, the charge and attested proof of an act of adultery. Divorce had routinely been a cause of peremptory banishment from Caroline Astor's favor, although, showing remarkable aplomb, she had once made an exception in the case of her headstrong daughter Charlotte Augusta, mother of four. Caroline managed to weather Charlotte's public embroilment in a steamy divorce brawl spiced with transatlantic flight, disinheritance, charges and countercharges of infidelity, and even the prospect of an old-fashioned duel in Paris between the lover and the outraged husband. Especially after her stroke, Caroline Astor's obedient son had been unwilling to put her to a further trial of this sort.

A year after his mother died, and following months of secret negotiations in the interim, he set in motion the machinery of divorce: by prior arrangement Ava sued him for a legal separation on grounds of adultery. Soon after, she won an interlocutory decree that gave her custody of six-year-old Alice, an annual allowance of $50,000, and an undisclosed settlement, rumored to be $2 million or $3 million, and possibly more. The settlement was in lieu of alimony, which would have required both parties to shed their cloaks of darkest secrecy and testify in open court. The smoothly silent way in which the Astors managed to get themselves severed by judicial fiat provoked at least as much public attention and protest as the divorce action itself. To prevent even a hint of the proceedings from seeping into public knowledge, eminent lawyers for both sides—Ava's was President Taft's brother—detached themselves for the occasion from corporate and estate responsibilities downtown, trooped up from their Wall Street offices, and filed the necessary papers in an out-of-the-way courtroom in New City, Rockland County. There, a state supreme court justice, Isaac Mills, heard the petition and referee's report, ordered the papers sealed, and declared the proceedings closed. Neither party to the divorce ever appeared in the courtroom or was mentioned by name. The identity of the correspondent (probably hired for the purpose) who alleged Jack's infidelities, the witness who corroborated them, and the place where these acts had occurred—none of these were ever disclosed. Not even the title of the case appeared on the sealed envelope containing the papers. Nothing was open to public inspection until the judge unsealed his decree, but not the papers supporting it. Defending the unusual secrecy, Mills denied, contrary to all appearances of favoritism and privilege, that Colonel and Mrs. Astor's power, money, and feelings had anything to do with the way he had arrived at his decision: he had only meant to protect the couple's two innocent children from the attentions of the tabloid press and its voracious readers. Names were not named, he tried to explain, because there was no need to name them.

CONTEMPT OF COURT, SECRET DIVORCE, GUMSHOE DIVORCE—there ensued a storm of editorial comment charging that the law had been perverted by wealth and influence; the guilty adulterer shielded from exposure and shame; and the rich favored over ordinary people, whose divorce actions on grounds of adultery were by custom laid out by the tabloid press in detail often lurid enough to corrupt the imagination of the young. "Never was a divorce proceeding made more thoroughly sound proof," said the *New York Globe.* "There was not the slightest leak. It takes experts to turn out such a job, and to experts it was confided." "In the Astor affair," the *Syracuse Herald* said, "not even the beginning of the suit was noted on the public record. Everything concerned with it was literally a 'sealed book.' . . . There is something radically amiss in any judicial system which favors the rich." "By what right," the *Richmond Times-Dispatch* said, "do our courts become so palpably respecters of persons? The law clearly contemplates publicity in divorce suits, as in others." According to the *New York Times,* a former justice of the state supreme court, Roger Pryor, claimed that "society was being injured a thousand times more by the spectacle of the rich and influential obtaining divorces in secret than by the publication of the testimony in divorce cases."

Both Astors remained far away from the turmoil of outrage as it slowly burned itself out into the customary acceptance of the fact that the very rich had special access to the ear of justice. The former Mrs. John Jacob Astor IV, under an assumed name—Mrs. Austin of Red Bank, New Jersey—secluded herself at French Lick Springs, a fashionable resort in Paoli, Indiana. A few days after the final decree came through she boarded the Cunard liner *Lusitania* and sailed for London. For years she had been a society fixture there, and her marital future was already being discussed, as if she were a horse entered at Ascot: Lord Curzon, until recently viceroy of India, was touted to be the front-runner among suitors for her hand. (The eventual winner was a wealthy sportsman, Lord Ribblesdale, Prime Minister Asquith's brother-in-law.)

Meanwhile Ava's former husband, along with their eighteen-year-old son Vincent, then a student at Harvard, and Vincent's companion, the future radio newsman H. V. Kaltenborn, had set off on a leisurely cruise in West Indian waters on board the *Nourmahal.* The Astor yacht was soon reported missing, presumably a casualty of a hurricane that was devastating Jamaica and other Caribbean islands and interrupting cable communications: the *Nourmahal* appeared to be adding dramatically to her long-standing reputation as a ship cursed with accidents. The vengeful god of storms ripped Colonel Astor from the privacy and isolation from the press he had managed to achieve during the divorce proceedings. For more than a week the *Nourmahal's* fate made front-page news with daily reports of its loss or survival. Searching the Caribbean was, in time, a fleet of ships, more than twenty in all, including U.S. Revenue cutters, a Royal Navy cruiser, a German navy cruiser, and a couple of banana steamers. The lead-story headlines grew in tempo and urgency:

ALARM FELT HERE FOR ASTOR YACHT;
MAY HAVE MET HURRICANE

ALARM GROWING OVER ASTOR YACHT

YACHT LIKE ASTOR'S SIGHTED ON SUNDAY;
FAR OUT OF HER COURSE

SEARCH SEAS FOR MISSING ASTOR YACHT;
ANXIETY HERE INCREASES

WRECK MAY BE ASTOR'S YACHT: GERMAN SHIP
REPORTS A SUBMERGED VESSEL NORTH OF MATANZAS, CUBA

And finally, a coda, hesitant at first:

REPORTS NOURMAHAL SAFE IN PORTO RICO;
NEWS COMES FROM CURACAO

DOUBT ASTOR YACHT IS SAFE AT SAN JUAN;
COMMUNICATION CUT OFF

ASTOR YACHT SAFE; IGNORANT OF ALARM

For ten days the *Nourmahal,* isolated from cable communication with the mainland, had been sheltered from the storm and safely anchored in San Juan Harbor. Meanwhile, unaware of any anxiety felt on their account, the owner and his party, riding in one of his big touring automobiles that he had shipped ahead from Ferncliff, had been taking in the sights of San Juan and Ponce. Soon after, as reported in the *Congressional Record,* the *Nourmahal* episode provoked a lively debate on the floor of the House of Representatives. A proposed resolution called for an accounting of the public money spent on the search for the yacht. According to opponents of the resolution, it appeared to insinuate that the Revenue Cutter Service subscribed to "a creed of snob-bishness" and might not have gone to the same trouble for a poor native's fishing vessel. One congressman managed to claim that the search had cost the Revenue Service little more than $60. "Even if Mr. Astor is a rich man," said another, citing Colonel Astor's services during the war with Spain, "he is deserving of much from the people of the United States." With the issue buried in a muddle of logic, it was decided to pass the resolution but en-sure that the proposed investigation be conducted "in a perfunc-tory way."

iv.

NO LONGER UNDER the thumb of two powerful women, his mother and his wife, the formerly withdrawn, gloomy, and belea-guered Colonel Astor became almost coltish. He had entered a new life under a new dispensation. He replaced the *Nourmahal* with a new yacht, the *Noma*. At enormous expense, he did over the white marble house on Fifth Avenue he had shared with his mother. He removed the partition wall between the two halves of the house. The space formerly occupied by twin staircases was now a bronze-domed reception hall exposing a vista that led past a great marble fireplace to a gold-ceilinged drawing room, a marble-columned dining room, a picture gallery, and the Astor ballroom, possibly the largest in the city. A portrait of old John Jacob As-tor, the long-ago source of this splendor, hung in the dining room. In the newly relocated library, shrinelike, hung the full-length Carolus-Duran portrait of Caroline Astor in front of which she had stood when receiving her guests. A year and a half after his mother died Jack gave a lavish housewarming party at 840 Fifth Avenue—a dinner dance for 250 guests—to announce to New York society that a new Astor generation now ruled the roost.

No longer reclusive, he accepted invitations to rounds of dinner dances, fancy-dress balls, weddings, auto shows, and other fashionable events. His name on guest lists appeared almost daily in the papers. With one of his sisters as hostess he entertained lavishly at the Fifth Avenue house and at Beechwood, his mother's "cottage" on Bellevue Avenue in Newport. More and more frequently he was to be seen in the company of a teenage girl he had met at Bar Harbor in the summer of 1910. He had apparently fallen in love with her right away. Madeleine Talmage Force, tall, strong-featured, pretty rather than beautiful, was a recent debutante and a graduate of Miss Spence's School for Girls. Having prospered in the shipping and forwarding business, William Force, her father, now a prominent sportsman and member of the New York Yacht Club, had moved his family from Remsen Street in Brooklyn to a house at 18 East Thirty-seventh Street in Manhattan. Madeleine's upwardly scrambling mother was known behind her back in society circles as "La Force Majeure."

When she and forty-six-year-old Jack Astor met, Madeleine was seventeen, considerably less than half his age, a year younger than his son, Vincent, and only about seven years older than his daughter, Alice. At first his friends tended to wave away this sudden, somewhat unsavory development as a passing infatuation on the part of a love-starved bachelor with an impressionable teenager who, unlike Ava, was responsive and dazzled by him. The gossip press exploited rumors of a possible or imminent engagement of a couple grotesquely disparate in their ages and in most quarters barred from marriage because the prospective groom was an accredited adulterer. "If Mr. Astor has found a woman willing to have him," said his divorced wife, by then comfortably settled in London society, "I do wish he would get married and drop out of the public prints; as he and I have nothing in common. I am sick and tired of it."

"Mother Force," the scandal sheet *Town Topics* soon reported, had "let no grass grow in getting her hook on the Colonel." This one-of-a-kind prospective son-in-law, an Astor of the Astors, was blessed with a fortune of over $100 million, a brand-new ocean-going steam yacht, and more hotels and skyscrapers than any other New Yorker. The Forces, mother and daughter, were soon regular guests in Astor's houses in New York, Ferncliff, and Newport; aboard the *Noma* traveling back and forth between New York and Newport; and in the Astor box, made famous by his mother, at the Metropolitan Opera. The Colonel and Madeleine were seen together so frequently that Father Force said he feared that such apparent intimacy, unless sanctified by a publicly avowed intention to marry, could lead to "unpleasant gossip" and the smutting of his virgin daughter's reputation. "I called Colonel Astor on the telephone today," Force told a reporter from the *Times,* "and we discussed the matter. He accepted my point of view, and it was agreed between us that I should make the announcement. No date has been set yet for the wedding." Having floated a gentle threat of a shotgun union, on August 1, 1911, Mr. and Mrs. William Force announced the engagement of their debutante daughter, Madeleine, to Colonel John Jacob Astor, great-grandson of John Jacob Astor and the recognized head of the Astor family in the United States.

Five weeks later, on September 9, following a desperate search for a clergyman willing to officiate, Astor and Madeleine were suddenly married by the Reverend Joseph Lambert, pastor of the

Elwood Temple Congregational Church of Providence, Rhode Island. Recruited on short notice and on payment of a fee of $1,000 (which the groom complained was extortionate), Lambert was about the only clergyman—and a Congregationalist at that, not a proper Episcopalian—who would agree to marry the pair. Lambert had been chosen over several other candidates who either volunteered or were scouted for the job, one of them a pastor in rural Tennessee, another an eighty-three-year-old Providence Baptist (and sometime spiritualist) who worked as a carpenter and occasionally picked up an odd dollar by performing ministerial duties. While the search was on, the Reverend Edward Johnson, a Newport Episcopalian, had turned down the $1,000 offer. "It was a lot of money to refuse and a big temptation to a poor minister, but I do not feel that I could marry the couple whatever was offered."

Half an hour after the couple exchanged vows the hastily arranged wedding breakfast was hastily consumed. The newlyweds left Beechwood by taxicab hired by a reporter (not expecting his services to be needed, Astor's chauffeur had taken the day off). They boarded the *Noma* and sailed out of Newport, cheered on by crowds of spectators gathered on the dock. Before he left, Astor released a curiously reasoned statement to the press. "Now that we are married," he said, "I don't care how difficult divorce and remarriage laws are made. I sympathize heartily with the most straitlaced people in most of their ideas, but believe remarriage should be possible once, as marriage is the happiest condition for the individual and the community."

The couple's opéra bouffe departure by ship left behind on shore the holiday-making crowd of local citizens along with members of the press hungry for details of what was instantly recognized as the most unusual marriage ever to take place in the high reaches of Newport. Also left behind was a clutch of Christian clergy embroiled in recriminations scarcely more dignified than a catfight. The rector of St. John's Episcopal Church in Philadelphia, who had earlier denounced the Astor-Force "alliance" as abhorrent, unholy, and in defiance of God's laws, now denounced his clerical brother, the Reverend Mr. Lambert, as a Judas who had taken a thousand pieces of silver to perform "a nasty job." He hoped Lambert would now "be driven from his sacred office and set to tending an Astor garage or cleaning an Astor stable." Another minister called Lambert "a disgrace to Congregationalism." "Of course, I can speak only for myself," said yet another, "but I unhesitatingly say that it was a shame and an outrage." Under fire from both fellow clergy and his parishioners for a sermon in which he defended the marriage, an Episcopal priest in Meriden, Connecticut, resigned his pulpit in disgust and said he was going into business instead.

Hot with disapproval of his union with a teenage girl they considered an arriviste, few of Astor's social peers, summoned on short notice, had attended the marriage ceremony at Beechwood. Little better attended were the entertainments Jack and Madeleine offered after returning from their honeymoon. To escape further snubs they spent the winter months of 1911–1912 traveling in Europe and enjoying the luxury of a houseboat on the Nile. When Madeleine learned she was pregnant they decided to cut short their stay abroad and come home. On April 10 they took the boat train from London's Victoria Station to Southampton and boarded the Royal Mail Steamer *Titanic*.

NINE

Baron Astor of Hever Castle

i.

WILLIAM WALDORF ASTOR turned sixty-four in 1912, the year his cousin Jack, unmourned by him, died on the *Titanic*. A peerage, which had been the height of William's ambition as a subject of Queen Victoria; her successor, King Edward VII; and, in turn, his successor, King George V, had continued to elude him. His old offenses against the dignity of the royal circle had never been forgotten; neither had his walling-off of Cliveden to keep the public out, resentment of the invasive power that came with the possession of millions of American dollars, and his opposition to the liberal policies of Prime Minister Herbert Asquith's government. "I was doing effective work all summer against Socialism," he wrote in 1909, "and believe I can be of use to my Conservative friends." Like his aunt Caroline, the late queen of New York society, but with a vehemence alien to her, he had appointed himself champion of aristocratic and regressive values.

More British than even the class-bound British establishment, he joined its battle against egalitarianism, reformist social change, and home rule for Ireland, the most divisive issue of the day. His chief weapon in the battle was the *Pall Mall Gazette*, a moderately liberal London evening paper he had acquired back in 1892, soon after moving to England. The conditions he laid on his appointed editor, Henry Cust, a former MP, were ominous and characteristic: "He shall at all times be bound by *any instructions and directions* which may be given him by the proprietor, whose right of *controlling the policy* and management of the paper are hereby acknowledged." Four years later, following disputes over policy and the handling—sometimes tactless rejection—of Astor's own contributions, he dismissed Cust. He then transformed this once openminded paper into what a historian of the Astor family, Derek Wilson, calls a "mouthpiece of the most reactionary elements in British politics." "Mr. Astor's paper," Wilson writes, "urged employers to stand firm against striking workers, advocated closing all museums and galleries to women in order to prevent sabotage by militant suffragettes, inveighed against attempts to engineer international armament reductions, resisted the imposition of death duties and estate taxes, and vociferously supported tariffs and imperial preference." The *Pall Mall Gazette*, William Waldorf Astor announced, was henceforth to be "written by gentlemen for gentlemen."

Several favored archetypes continued to shape Astor's bristling and conflicted but, as sometimes observed from the outside, vulnerable nature. One was the honest peasant of Baden who sprang fresh from the soil and, endowed with the genius of trade and modern capitalism, went on to amass one of the great fortunes of his time. In William's imagination, the commoner John Jacob Astor, canny dealer in pelts and house lots, contended for mastery with the fictive Spanish Crusader of noble blood who fell at the siege of Jerusalem. The Crusader generally won out. Sometimes Astor also thought of himself as Aladdin, possessor and bestower of magic wealth. In his tender moments he liked to think of himself, too, as the amorous creature of Stéphane Mallarmé's famous poem, "L'Après-Midi d'un faune."

"One's heart just cries out for that poor old gentleman," his daughter-in-law, the former Nancy Langhorne of Virginia, was to say of William after his death in 1919. "Had he been born with 2 sous, I feel, [he] would have become a great man." Wealth, and the sense of privilege that came with it, had molded his character and given even his most apparently benign gestures a hint of self-serving and appropriation. His gift to Nancy, when she married his eldest son, Waldorf, in 1906, was the 55.23 carat Sancy diamond, a historic stone that during the past several centuries had supposedly passed through the hands of Charles the Bold, two kings of England, Louis XIV, and the czars of Russia. What William gave to his son was equally spectacular: the entire Cliveden estate along with all its decorations and furnishings, its sculptures and busts, Roman sarcophagi, enormous wine jars, funerary urns, suits of armor, and other antiquities collected over the years. "The most magnificent wedding gift ever made, I should imagine," William called it. Pharaonic in their grandeur, such gifts coming from William as Aladdin could be received as acts of self-commemoration and even aggression. They overwhelmed their recipients and threatened to bend them to the giver's personality.

Lying ill at his office on Victoria Embankment with a severe attack of gout, William did not attend the wedding ceremony of Waldorf and Nancy. Although civil and even affectionate, the accommodation he subsequently reached with his sharp-tongued daughter-in-law proved to be at best a sort of negotiated truce. The most effectual and vivid of the modern Astors, she was William's equal if not his superior in opinionatedness and intelligence. "I married beneath me," she said in a famous quip. "All women do."

She was the first woman to win election to a seat in the House of Commons. A battery of rockets liable to go off in many directions at once, she differed with her father-in-law on virtually every question that could be raised between them. That she was an American previously married and divorced was among the tender points, along with her stand on social justice and women's rights. He hardly tried to hide his exasperation at her egalitarian positions, her outspoken role as a Christian Science evangelist, and her ban on alcoholic beverages at Cliveden (and, if she had her way, in all of Britain). The renovations Nancy Astor ordered when she became chatelaine of Cliveden undid both the substance and the spirit of William's most cherished possession. He had poured into the house and grounds the same passion for burnished splendor that shaped his hotels and his other private residences. Once installed at Cliveden the young Astors set about changing its feel and style. "The keynote of the place when I took over was splendid gloom," Nancy recalled. "Tapestries and ancient leather furniture filled most of the rooms. The place looked better when I had put in books and chintz curtains and covers, and flowers." She ripped out one of William's prized installations, the mosaic stone floor in the main hall, and replaced it with a more welcoming and more fashionable parquet. She replaced the Italian-style dining-room ceiling that had been painted to William's order and cleared out his collection of Roman sarcophagi, stone sculptures, suits of armor, funerary urns, and antique Italian furniture. She changed the Cliveden of "splendid gloom" and long history into a grand English country house where she was to play hostess to Winston Churchill, T. E. Lawrence, Charlie Chaplin, and other grandees of her day.

"I prefer to remember things as I left them," William said soon after handing Cliveden over to Waldorf and Nancy and moving out for good. Resigned to changes the new owners were bound to make, he intended never even to visit, but when he did visit he was appalled. Dreading his response to her improvements, Nancy took to her bed when she heard his car arrive and deliver him for a visit. "The house has been somewhat altered in decoration and furniture," he later noted, drily enough, considering his dismay, "and without objecting to these changes, it is no pleasure for me to see them."

Hever Castle was now his summer home, but he intended to spend the remaining winter months of his life in Italy. This was William's country of romance. He had first seen Naples in 1855 at the age of seven, when Bourbon king Ferdinand II ruled the Two Sicilies. Later he had fallen in love in Italy for the first time and dreamed of living a life there devoted to writing, sculpture, and study, only to go home, with a regret that never lessened, to take up his business duties as an Astor. Still later, married by then, he spent three fulfilling years in Rome as U.S. minister. The year before he handed Cliveden over to his son, he bought a property in Sorrento, overlooking the Gulf of Naples and within sight of Vesuvius and Pompeii. "Sorrento is a place I have known and delighted in for thirty-five years," he wrote to Amy Richardson, "and so far as beauty is concerned it is as near Paradise as anything I expect to see."

His new possession was a three-story nineteenth-century building on an estate that he named Sirena after the Greek sea nymphs whose song was supposed to have lured mariners to their island. Extending the property with an acre and a half of cloister garden and orange grove, he bought and tore down an adjacent church and monastery. Sirena was the last of his grand acquisitions and offered him the chance to enjoy an even deeper, more thorough immersion in the distant past than his historical fiction and his restorations at Cliveden and Hever Castle. Child of the century of steel, steam, electricity, and America's leap to world power, he tried to create at Sorrento an alternative world bathed in the light of the Roman Empire at high noon.

At a cost of half a million dollars, and after about two years of work, Astor constructed on the property an adjoining villa of a sort that might have been owned and inhabited by a patrician Roman family in the first century BC. He had decided to do this after his workmen uncovered among ruins in the garden a marble altar inscribed with the names of the villa's first occupants. In the excavation and construction that followed he drew on his own respectable knowledge of classical culture. He ordered shipped over from England a "Noah's Ark," as he called it, of marbles and bronzes he had been keeping in storage. He hired scholars and artists to scour Europe's markets and private collections for authentic period furnishings, painted decorations for the stucco walls, and mosaic pieces for the tessera floors. Twenty-four red and white marble columns with antique Corinthian capitals lined the court leading to the villa's inner rooms. Each, a visitor wrote, was "furnished in the Roman style, with marble tables and bronze candlesticks . . . and with arm chairs in marble." The villa's wine cellar held Greek and Roman amphorae found during excavation of the grounds. The kitchen was equipped with antique earthenware bottles and dishes, iron stew pans and gridirons, a mill for grinding grain, and a bronze mortar. Six stone lions' heads supported an antique dining table ringed with bronze chairs covered with rough bear and wolf skins.

ii.

OVER THE YEARS, Astor had entertained unnamed women friends in his "studio," a private apartment at his Temple Place office, and in his "secluded retreat" at Hever, to which only he had the key. Once or twice, and unreliably, he had been linked romantically with various titled or socially prominent women, but for the most part this was rumor only and short-lived. Dreading the attentions of the press, he managed to conduct his casual affairs without a hint of scandal, a remarkable achievement given his money, which drew inquiring reporters like flies to honey, and the fact that practically everything else about this richest of rich marriage prospects was newsworthy, even his arrivals, departures, and silences. In conducting his affairs with such discretion he had in mind the contrary example of his cousin Jack, who had seemed often to be living his private life under a noonday sun of publicity.

Sixty-five in 1913, a widower for seventeen years, William contracted a grand passion. There may have been others since his Italian romance decades back, but this one left behind in its eventual wreckage a trail of love letters that showed him in an unfamiliar light. The forbidding and withdrawn William Waldorf Astor felt young again and imagined himself Faun, Aladdin, and Don Giovanni as well. He had fallen in love with Lady Victoria Sackville, a celebrated beauty and charmer. Fifty-one, she had perfect skin, captivating eyes, knee-length silken hair, and an engaging foreignness acquired at the French convent where she had been educated and also inherited from her mother, a Spanish dancer named Pepita, who had borne her out of wedlock. Victoria's father was the British minister to the United States. As British as she was

Continental, on both her father's side and her husband's Victoria claimed descent from a hero of the Battle of Crécy in 1346. "There is no end to your perfections. . . . You are an accomplished mistress in love," one of this Circe's long-standing captives, the British diplomat Cecil Spring-Rice, wrote to her. "You play with it and use it and manage it, like a seagull the wind, on which he floats but is never carried away."

Accustomed to being the object of fervent but often unrequited adoration, Victoria saw herself as the heroine of a popular novel, perhaps by Dumas père or Ouida. "Quel roman est ma vie!" she said. But she also had a hard head for business, especially in dealings that involved paintings and tapestries. With her talent for both love and money she would have been at home in the France of the *Grandes Horizontales*. She conducted serial, sometimes overlapping affairs while leading a mostly separate life from her husband (and cousin), Lionel Sackville-West, heir to a sprawling Elizabethan estate, Knole at Sevenoaks, in Kent. It had been in his family since 1603 and was now chronically strapped for cash because of new tax laws and rising labor costs to maintain its spectacular gardens. According to her grandson, Nigel Nicolson, Victoria practically cornered the market in "millionaires and lonely elderly artists." Among her conquests were Auguste Rodin; Field Marshal Lord Kitchener, the hero of Khartoum; department store magnate H. Gordon Selfridge; and William Waldorf Astor's immediate predecessor in her favors, Pierpont Morgan, then seventy-four.

"He holds my hand with much affection," Victoria wrote in her diary after a tête-à-tête with Morgan, "and says he will never care for me in any way I would not approve of, that he was sorry to be so old, but I was the one woman he loved and he would

never change." "I have never met anyone so attractive," she wrote
a few days later. She found Morgan so attractive, she said, that she
managed to ignore his famous swollen nose, ravaged by acne
rosacea and glowing like a railroad signal lamp. She had a business
as well as a romantic relationship with Morgan, to whom she sold
off some of the heirlooms at Knole to raise cash for maintenance.
Soon after Morgan's death in 1913 Victoria took William Waldorf
Astor in tow.

"A woman in the flower of her prime—like yourself—needs a romantic attachment," William wrote to her from Marienbad, where
he had gone to take the waters for his gout and rheumatism. "Without it the heart grows cold. It is as necessary as daily bread, and
not even Knole and four acres at Hampstead can take its place. It
is the consciousness that someone is thinking of you, desires you,
longs for the touch of your beautiful body that keeps the heart
young. Sweetheart, goodbye." He signed himself "Will." He confessed that for years when they met socially he had been afraid of
her, "by which I mean fearful of displeasing you, for to have done
so would have pained me dreadfully."

Everything between them had changed one afternoon—he
called it his own "après-midi d'un faun"—when she came to see
him in his "secluded retreat" at Hever Castle. "Have just come in
for a walk," he wrote after she left. "I smiled to notice the foot-
prints, large and small, in the wet gravel at the House of the Poetic
Faun . . . for anything I might have said and done in that splendid
hour's excitement I entreat forgiveness. . . . I take away with me an
infinitely delightful remembrance, and I kiss your hand." Later he
added, "That momentous Saturday was the psychological hour for
which you and I have unconsciously waited. . . . What wonderful
things awaken at the meeting of the hands." He urged her to come

to him again for lunch and the afternoon. "The only suitable rendezvous I know of in England is my office, a little palace on the Embankment where I live in solitude. *La ci darem la mano!* Without at present attempting details I would show you how to arrive veiled and unannounced and as I alone should let you in and out, none but we could know." Fooley, his butler-valet, he assured her, "has been with me 13 years. He has seen many things and has always been discreet."

Victoria declined the invitation, but teased him with the prospect of a chaperoned and chaste meeting in Switzerland, what she called "a picnic without refreshments." Resigned to her proposed regimen of "iced love-making," he said he would be happy, nevertheless, "to take your dear hand in mine again. . . . I shall have no other thought than to please you in all things." In his love-struck Aladdin mode he had prevailed on her to accept from him "a little gift" of £10,000 in banknotes for the garden at Knole.

By the end of the winter of 1913–1914, though, Astor had been replaced in Victoria's affections by a former lover, a Swedish baron, whom she ran into in Perugia on her way to visit Astor in Sorrento. The baron had unexpectedly resurfaced in her life after an absence of thirty-two years, exerted his old powers, and "won me again entirely," she wrote in her diary. Traveling by her chauffeured Rolls-Royce, she then proceeded south to Sorrento to break the news to Astor. After a weekend at Villa Sirena, the affair with him that she had managed with discretion and restraint—always "careful not to be talked about"—was pronounced dead, having suffered internal injuries on the way there. "He seems disappointed in me. What else can I do?" Victoria wrote in her diary. "We are parting perfectly good friends, but things have changed, alas." From then on her loving "Will" signed his letters to her

"W. W. Astor." "He has become so hard on everybody," she wrote in her diary, "even against his own children, and so self-centered and unfeeling about everything."

For a year he had set aside his old self, and when his affair with Lady Sackville was over he began to shut down as if in preparation for his demise. He divested himself of his publishing enterprises. He conveyed to his sons, Waldorf and John Jacob V, all of his holdings in Manhattan real estate. Assessed at about $70 million, they included the northern part of the Broadway frontage formerly occupied by his ancestor's Astor House, the Waldorf section of the Waldorf-Astoria, the Hotel Astor, the Astor Theater, the Astor Court Building, the Astor Apartments, and the New Netherland Hotel, along with a number of office buildings and apartment houses that without blazoning the Astor name nevertheless asserted the Astor primacy on Manhattan Island.

The driving force in William's final years remained the determination to win a place in the British peerage. He made no secret of his ambition, even at the cost of inviting ridicule. Once, without having received any signal to justify his confidence that the day of his elevation was at hand, he appeared at a party wearing a peer's ermine-and-velvet robe. What he believed was the holy grail of a title, more down-to-earth and realistic folk recognized as being in many cases a crass recognition of successes in commodities such as beer, soap, and cereal, and of generous contributions to party coffers. In the spirit that drove his quest he had more in common with his former countrymen than he would have liked to acknowledge: instead of comporting themselves like citizens of a democracy that had shaken off aristocratic distinctions, Americans were notorious for becoming virtually unhinged with borrowed glory when they found themselves shaking hands with a duke. Even more than the cooked-up genealogy William had commissioned, the prospect of becoming Lord Astor was a preemptive way to at least mitigate the fact of his descent from the soil of Baden.

Before 1914, when England entered the war, and especially after, he made large gifts to the Conservative Party that were duly noted by the dispensers of royal favor: he also gave $250,000 to the universities, and during the war $275,000 to various charities and hospitals, $200,000 to the Red Cross, and $175,000 to a public fund for the wounded. Counting in his "war loans" and outright personal gifts, he may have given away as much as $5 million. "It must have been a great deal more fun to make money and spend most of it on the public, as Mr. Carnegie did," the *New York Times* commented when Astor finally achieved his peerage, "than to be born rich and then try to make your way to other distinctions."

After a decade of benefactions bolstered by direct and indirect politicking, William was at last named a peer of the realm on King George V's New Year's Day Honors list in 1916. Two weeks later, robed as Baron Astor of Hever Castle, he made a twenty-minute pro forma appearance in the House of Lords. He reappeared there the following year when he was upped a notch to viscount. Meanwhile he carried on an extensive correspondence with the College of Arms and the editors of Debrett's *Peerage* on the subject of the heraldic device to replace the one on his pre-peerage flag. After drafts and redrafts he settled on the motto *Ad Astra* and the emblem of a falcon surmounted by an eagle and three stars and flanked by two standing figures, an American Indian and a fur trapper, altogether a conflation of Astor family history, both true and imagined.

Astor's elder son, Waldorf, was already well launched on a career in politics as member of Parliament for Plymouth. He did not welcome his father's elevation to the peerage. For him a hereditary title in the Astor family, far from being a desirable distinction, was a disaster, even a stigma to be passed on by law from father to son: by law, on William's death Waldorf would have to resign his elected seat and, against his will, move to the relatively ineffectual House of Lords as the second Viscount Astor. Displaying a remarkable lack of empathy, he demanded that William renounce his hard-won title. That failing, he threatened to find a legal way to relinquish it when it passed to him. In his father's view all this was not only an impossible demand but an unpardonable insult. "I am sorry that Waldorf takes my promotion so bitterly hard," William wrote to his daughter-in-law, Nancy. "I cannot think that what has happened is in any sense a decadence and the course of advancement is as open to me as to him. . . . The love of success is in my blood, and personally speaking I am delighted to have rounded these last years of my life with a distinction." "I have never gone in pursuit of this honor," the first Viscount Astor added, possibly having convinced himself, while in the grip of denial, that this was conceivably the case. "In all things the honor should come to the man and not that the man should go stalking the honor." He banished Waldorf, and during the three years before William's death, they never spoke to each other.

William's relationship with Waldorf's sister, Pauline, was equally contentious and as brutally terminated. She had tried to mediate the quarrel over title and succession only to be similarly banished as a party to her brother's insulting behavior. Even much later, although suffering from progressive heart disease and chronic gout and declining into invalidism, William rejected an offer from Pauline to nurse and companion him. "I told you three years ago," he wrote, "that I did not wish to see you again. There is no reason for me to change my mind." "I pity my father from the bottom of my heart," Pauline said, "and think it's almost impossible for us to realize the emptiness and the misery of the life he has made for himself." Viscount Astor was now alienated from two of his three children. He had given over Hever to the third, John Jacob V, recuperating there from war wounds and the partial amputation of his right leg.

Soon after his elevation to viscount and his move from Hever, Astor went into seclusion in a house at Brighton, on the Sussex coast. He had long been fond of this favored resort of royalty and believed the sea air would act as a cure. Recently redecorated for him in the Astor manner, the last of his houses was an otherwise undistinguished two-story Regency building at 155 King's Road, almost across the way from the Edward VII memorial. Occupied by a reclusive millionaire, a famous former American recently raised to the peerage, Astor's silent retreat became one of the mysteries and curiosities of Brighton. A high board fence surrounded the property and blocked views from the outside. Astor's butler and a private detective patrolled the perimeter and guarded the front gate, turning away anyone who applied for admission. Not even the borough surveyor was permitted to enter to exercise his official function.

On the evening of October 18, 1919, Astor sat down alone to his customary four-course dinner prepared to his orders by a resident cook and accompanied by wines from his cellar. After taking coffee and port he withdrew behind the closed door of his lavatory and died there. The cause of his death at the age of seventy-one and a half was probably congestive heart failure. London and New York papers the next day were skittish in accounting for the precise location of his demise, it being more in keeping with both

journalistic decorum in dealing with the dead and the dignity of
the dead viscount to report that he had died in bed instead of on
the toilet. After simple services in London attended by Astor's
three children and their spouses the body was cremated, and, following standing instructions, the ashes were buried under the marble floor of the private chapel he had prepared at Cliveden.

Two years before he died, Astor had printed for himself and a
few friends a seventy-six-page book of reminiscences, *Silhouettes:
1855–1885.* There he recalled his boyhood in New York; his parents'
stifling religious orthodoxy from which, at the age of eighteen, he
liberated himself; his training at the Astor estate office; his careers
in politics and diplomacy; and, most poignant of all his memories,
the Italian girl—"the Princess of my fairy tale"—whom he had not
been allowed to marry. For all his contrary and agitated nature, he
even managed to claim for himself the achievement of "a peace
the classics knew," a peace that was surely unsuspected by his children and others who had run up against his will. Turning to the literature of his native country, and to perhaps its most passionate
celebrator of democracy, nativism, and solitude, he prefaced his
book with a passage from *Leaves of Grass.* Walt Whitman's lines
spoke as well for William's own longing for equanimity:

> I think I could turn and live with animals; they are so
>   placid and self-contained;
> I stand and look at them long and long.
> They do not sweat and whine about their condition;
> They do not lie awake in the dark and weep for their
>   sins.
> They do not make me sick discussing their duty to God.

TEN

End of the Line

*K*NOWN NATIONWIDE as "the Forty-second Street Country Club," the popular bar in Jack Astor's Hotel Knickerbocker on Times Square became a casualty of Prohibition in 1919. When it closed, it took the hotel down with it. In May 1929, five months before the stock market crash of Black Tuesday marked the end of good times, the Waldorf-Astoria, for four decades site, symbol, and catalyst of that era, also closed its doors. By Jazz Age standards its style and grandeur were stodgy, snobbish, and out of date. Relatively remote from the stretch of fashionable New York along upper Fifth Avenue, the hotel had also been hit by ten years of Prohibition that effectively shut off a major source of income and traffic. Reflective visitors who thronged the lobby and corridors during the hotel's last days in business recalled the dreams of wealth, luxury, glamour, and proximity to the great and famous that had been played out there. They visited for the last time the silken, velvet, and marble settings of Peacock Alley, the Turkish Salon, the Palm Court Restaurant, and the grand ballroom.

Closing-night entertainment in the ballroom was far from being one of the extravaganzas for which the hotel had been celebrated. The event was homelier, more in keeping with the coming era of the Depression: a performance by the one hundred members of the Consolidated Gas and Electric Choral Society. In the record three-week-long on-site auction that followed the closing, souvenir collectors, sentimentalists, antiquarians, and dealers bid on more than twenty thousand lots of hotel property. The auction inventory included bath mats and towels lettered "W.A.," brass spittoons (destined to be recycled for use as fern bowls), chairs, dishes, bric-a-brac, 125 pianos, and other items down to the last spoon, finger bowl, and wine goblet. The world-famous name "Waldorf-Astoria," which encapsulated the history of both an era and a dynasty, went for a token $1 to the builders of a new and otherwise unrelated hotel going up on Park Avenue. By February 1930 Henry Hardenbergh's great building, one of the architectural wonders of Manhattan, had been leveled. Its two-acre site, where the parents of the Astor cousins once dwelt in their brownstone mansions, was cleared for another architectural milestone, the 102-story Empire State Building.

In a comparably radical transition from the old order to the new, the marble chateau at 840 Fifth Avenue where Caroline Astor and her son Jack had assembled the chosen in the ballroom, had also yielded to Manhattan's inexorable tide of demolition, renewal, and social change. Torn down in the 1920s, the Astors' mansion was replaced by Temple Emanu-El, one of the world's largest synagogues and both symbol and assembly place of Manhattan's new Jewish hegemony.

In 1967, along with the Metropolitan Opera House, a similar monument of a bygone era, the spectacular Hotel Astor fell to the wreckers. Workmen said it was the most difficult job of its sort they had ever known: the walls were so fortress-thick that the massive iron ball of the demolition crane often brought down nothing but chips of masonry and clouds of dust. Meanwhile, the surrounding theater district, the *Times* reported, had become "standee country for viewers of one of the smash hits in town—the demolition of the Astor Hotel." A towering office building went up in its place. "Meet me at the Astor," a New York byword, was now a whisper from the past. In 1926, on the site of William Waldorf Astor's once-commanding New Netherland rose the Sherry-Netherland Hotel, a thirty-eight-story building more than twice as high as the one it replaced and topped with a slender spire. During the 1990s, having long since passed out of the Astor estate into corporate ownership, Jack's St. Regis underwent what was said to be a $100 million makeover that modernized and at the same time restored it to its original gilded, bronze, and marble splendor.

Along with his villa at Sorrento, William Waldorf Astor's Hever Castle, his "House of the Poetic Faun," likewise passed into outside hands. In 1982 his grandson Gavin Astor put Hever up for sale (at $25 million) after a series of floods turned the property surrounding the castle into a giant moat. At last report, the current owners, Broadland Properties Limited, operate Hever as a combined conference center and theme park. Visitors can buy tickets for admission to the castle, gardens, maze of yew hedge, topiary, and the former owner's collections of Roman statuary, arms and armor, and "historic instruments of execution, torture, and discipline" (the last a powerful attraction for the young). Hever also offers special events like a Royal Jousting Tournament, a demonstration of Tudor archery, and a festival of autumn colors. Astor's Anne Boleyn relics are still in place, an essential element, the proprietors say, in the castle's "homely atmosphere." The Tudor village Astor designed to accommodate his guests and staff while he lived alone in his moated castle is now "an exclusive-use venue with twenty-five bedrooms and is used for corporate events and private dining throughout the year." A few years after his death Astor's office building at 2 Temple Place went to an insurance company for use as corporate headquarters. Damaged in the bombing of London during World War II and afterward repaired, Temple Place is now a conference center. The weather vane Astor designed for his London retreat, a golden replica of one of Columbus's caravels, still turns in the wind.

Together, and also in competition with each other, the two Astor cousins had enriched hotel life, social life, and even civic life on the American continent. In doing this they had asserted personal pride and an unshakable sense of superiority derived from great wealth and the loose definition of aristocracy that Americans have always favored. Even though he had made a gift of it to his son, it was the estate at Cliveden that closed the circle on William's own life and on a career, like his cousin's, as innkeeper on an imperial scale. William's statue of a wounded Amazon, emblem of his youthful ambition to escape the family countinghouse, still stands in the rose garden he commissioned. He had brought over to Cliveden and installed above the parterre the monumental stone balustrade from the Borghese garden in Rome acquired during his term as American minister. Impassive and commanding, William Waldorf Astor himself looks out from Von Herkomer's portrait in oils that hangs above the marble mantelpiece in the dining room. His ashes are buried beneath the chapel floor. Even after the radical changes in style and atmosphere that his daughter-in-law had ordered, Cliveden bears his signature and expresses his determination to reconstitute himself as a Briton and commemorate himself by possessing one of the stately homes of England.

Cliveden's subsequent history would have dismayed William.

In the fall of 1937 Claud Cockburn, a member of the British Communist Party and editor of the influential single-sheet news bulletin the *Week,* wrote a story about what came to be known as "the Cliveden Set." According to Cockburn, this was a clutch of highly placed Britons, some of them prominent in public life, who supported Hitler, favored accommodation to the Third Reich, and hoped to shape their own government's policy accordingly. In effect (or at least intention) Cliveden had become the seat of "Britain's second Foreign Office." According to Cockburn, members of this cabal met on long country weekends at the Astor estate and laid their plans there with Hitler's representatives. (The British novelist Kazuo Ishiguro's 1989 novel *The Remains of the Day* presents a highly colored version of these conferences at Cliveden, renamed "Darlington Hall.") During the anxious months before German tanks rolled into Poland, the notion of a "Cliveden Set," however much it had been a product of Cockburn's flair for the sensational, captured the public imaginings and provoked alarming news reports. "Friends of Hitler strong in Britain," the *New York Times* reported from London. "The apparent strength of Germany's case in this country comes from the fact that Germany's best friends are to be found in the wealthiest 'upper crust' of British life." In all likelihood, according to a recent study (Norman Rose, *The Cliveden Set* [London, 2000]), Cockburn's sinister "Cliveden Set" was a more or less harmless think tank composed of amateurs, misguided do-gooders, and busybodies who were, as Ishiguro's novel suggests, "out of their depth."

Cockburn's story and its sequels left a permanent smudge on the reputations of Nancy Astor and her husband, Waldorf, hosts and organizers of the Cliveden weekends. Otherwise outspoken chiefly on the subject of racehorses, Astor published a long letter to the *Times* of London in which he denounced Cockburn's article as "a Communist fiction," "a myth from beginning to end." He charged that it maliciously conflated a well-intentioned policy of exploring avenues to peace with active support of Adolf Hitler. But the damage had been done: Cliveden, William Waldorf Astor's retreat in the English countryside, was to be remembered as a nest of vipers. For his part, Cockburn was delighted by the immediate and lasting currency of the phrase he coined. "People who wanted to explain everything by something and were ashamed to say 'sunspots,' " he wrote in his memoirs, "said 'Cliveden Set.' "

In the early 1960s, during the cold war between the West and Khrushchev's Soviet Union, the name Cliveden gained further notoriety. A private poolside party there was the source of a scandal that involved an alleged breach of national security and caused the eventual fall of Prime Minister Harold Macmillan's government. Possibly inspired by the *Fountain of Love* statuary group William Waldorf Astor had installed along the grand avenue leading to the house, a teenage call girl named Christine Keeler shed her clothes, danced naked about the Cliveden pool, and engaged the fancy of two party guests in particular. Each of them, concurrently, became her lover. One was John Profumo, Macmillan's minister for war, and the other was Captain Eugene Ivanov, a Soviet intelligence agent whose official cover was military attaché. Guilty of lying about the affair to the House of Commons, Profumo left his cabinet post in disgrace. "Profumo Affair" became as firmly fastened to Cliveden as Cockburn's unsquelchable phrase.

Britain's National Trust now owns the Cliveden property and its 375 acres of lawn, gardens, and woodland. During the 1970s the trust leased Cliveden to Stanford University, and subsequently to

the University of Massachusetts, for use as an overseas study center for undergraduates—as it turned out, an awkward experiment in
disparate living styles. The manor at Cliveden now operates as a
luxury hotel that outdoes the prototypical New York establishments of more than a century earlier. Including butler, footmen,
housemaids, and cooks, the hotel at Cliveden claims to employ a
staff of four for each of its thirty-seven bedrooms. It's the right
place for those who, like its former owner, wish to live like a lord
and can afford it.

ACKNOWLEDGMENTS

For their encouragement and support I thank my literary agent of many years, Sterling Lord, and at Viking, my vigilant editor Wendy Wolf and her assistant Clifford Corcoran. Maggie Berkvist proved to be the Kit Carson of picture scouts. Many thanks to my old friends Marilyn McCully and Michael Raeburn for their hospitality in London and for a memorable visit to Cliveden. For courtesies along the way I'm also grateful to Daniel Aaron, John Y. Cole, and the staffs at Harvard University Archives, Harvard College Library, and manuscript collections at the Library of Congress and the New York Public Library. My deepest indebtedness is to my wife, novelist Anne Bernays, for her patient readings of the manuscript and invaluable editorial advice.

Sources

Unless otherwise noted, place of publication is New York.

Akin, Edward M. *Flagler: Rockefeller Partner and Florida Baron.* Kent, Ohio, 1988.

Alsop, Susan Mary. *Lady Sackville.* 1978.

Astor Family Papers. Special Collections, New York Public Library.

Astor, John Jacob, IV. *A Journey in Other Worlds: A Romance of the Future.* 1894.

Astor, Michael. *Tribal Feeling.* London, 1963.

Astor, William Waldorf. "John Jacob Astor." *Pall Mall Magazine,* June 1899.

Astor, William Waldorf, Papers. Library of Congress, Washington, D.C.

Astor, William Waldorf. *Pharaoh's Daughter and Other Stories.* 1900.

——. *Sforza, a Story of Milano.* 1889.

——. *Silhouettes: 1855–1885.* London, 1917.

——. *Valentino: An Historical Romance of the Sixteenth Century in Italy.* 1885.

Bach, Richard F. "Henry Janeway Hardenbergh." *Architectural Record,* July 1918.

Baum, Vicki. *Grand Hotel.* 1931.

Bellamy, Edward. *Looking Backward 2000–1887.* 1888.

Biel, Steven. *Down with the Old Canoe.* 1996.

Bourget, Paul. *Outre-mer: Impressions of America.* 1895.

Cather, Willa. *The Troll Garden.* 1905.

Chandler, David L. *Henry Flagler.* 1986.

Cowles, Virginia. *The Astors.* 1979.

Crockett, Albert Stevens. *Peacocks on Parade.* 1931.

David, Arthur C. "The Boot Type of Metropolitan Hotel." *Architectural Record,* June 1904.

Dreiser, Theodore. *An American Tragedy*. 1925.

——. *Sister Carrie*. Philadelphia, 1900.

Duffus, Mary McDowell, Lady Hardy. *Through Cities and Prairie Lands*. 1881.

Eliot, William Havard. *A Description of the Tremont House, with Architectural Illustrations*. Boston, 1830.

Fenster, J. M. "Palaces of the People." *American Heritage*, April 1994.

Girouard, Mark. *The Victorian Country House*. 1979.

Harvard University Archives, Cambridge, Mass.

Homberger, Eric. *The Historical Atlas of New York City*. 1994.

——. *Mrs. Astor's New York*. New Haven, Conn., 2002.

Hone, Philip. *The Diary of Philip Hone, 1828–1851*. Edited by Allan Nevins. 1927.

Hotel Astor, Indian Hall. Promotional brochure, 1904.

Hotel Astor, Times Square, New York. Promotional brochure, 1904.

Hungerford, Edward. *The Story of the Waldorf-Astoria*. 1925.

Irving, Washington. *Astoria*. 1836.

James, Henry. *The American Scene*. 1907.

—— *Daisy Miller*. 1878.

——. *The Finer Grain*. 1910.

Kavaler, Lucy. *The Astors*. 1966.

Kipling, Rudyard. *American Notes*. Norman, Okla., 1981.

——. *From Sea to Sea*. 1899.

Lapidus, Morris. *An Architecture of Joy*. Miami, 1979.

——. *Too Much Is Never Enough*. 1996.

Lehr, Elizabeth Drexel. *"King Lehr" and the Gilded Age*. Philadelphia, 1935.

Leng, John. *America in 1876*. Dundee, Scotland, 1877.

Logan, Andy. *The Man Who Robbed the Robber Barons*. 1965.

Mann, William D'Alton, ed. *Fads and Fashions of Representative Americans at the Beginning of the Twentieth Century*. 1905.

Martin, Frederick Townsend. *The Passing of the Idle Rich*. 1911.

——. *Things I Remember*. 1913.

Martin, Ralph G. *Jennie*. Englewood Cliffs, N.J., 1969.

Martin, Sidney Walter. *Florida's Flagler*. Athens, Ga., 1949.

Mayer, Grace. *Once Upon a City*. 1967.

Millhauser, Stephen. *Martin Dressler*. 1996.

Morehouse, Ward. *The Waldorf-Astoria*. 1991.

Morris, Lloyd. *Incredible New York*. 1951.

Myers, Gustavus. *History of the Great American Fortunes*. 1937.

Nevill, Dorothy. *Under Five Reigns*. London, 1910.

Nicolson, Nigel. *Portrait of a Marriage*. 1973.

O'Connor, Harvey. *The Astors*. 1941.

Pall Mall Magazine, 1897–1901.

Parton, James. "John Jacob Astor." *Harper's New Monthly Magazine* 30 (1865).

Porter, Kenneth Wiggins. *John Jacob Astor*. 1931.

Ronda, James P. *Astoria and Empire*. Lincoln, Neb., 1990.

Ross, Ishbel. *Silhouette in Diamonds*. 1960.

The St. Regis Hotel. Promotional brochure, 1905.

Schuyler, Montgomery. "Henry Janeway Hardenbergh." *Architectural Record*, March 1897.

Silver, Nathan. *Lost New York*. Boston, 1967.

Sinclair, David. *Dynasty: The Astors and Their Times*. London, 1993.

Smith, Horace Herbert. *Crooks of the Waldorf*. 1929.

Smith, Matthew Hale. *Sunshine and Shadow in New York*. 1869.

Spann, Edward K. *The New Metropolis: New York City, 1840–1857*. 1981.

Stern, Robert A. M., Gregory Gilmartin and John Massengale. *New York 1900*. 1983.

——, Gregory Gilmartin and Thomas Mellins. *New York 1930*. 1987.

Stewart, Robert. "The Hotels of New York." *Munsey's*, November 1899.

Strong, George Templeton. *The Diary of George Templeton Strong*. Edited by Allan Nevins and Milton Halsey Thomas. 1952.

Strouse, Jean. *Morgan*. 1999.

Sykes, Christopher. *Nancy: The Life of Lady Astor*. 1972.

New York Times, 1857–.

Town Topics, 1896–1897.

Trollope, Anthony. *North America*. 1951.

Wells, H. G. *The Future in America*. 1906.

Wharton, Edith. *The Custom of the Country*. 1913.

——. *Certain People*. 1930.

White, Arthur. *Palaces of the People*. London, 1968.

Williamson, Jefferson. *The American Hotel*. 1930.

Wilson, Derek. *The Astors: Landscape with Millionaires*. 1993.

Zeisloft, E. I., ed. *The New Metropolis*. 1899.

INDEX